W9-CPB-800

Yes, Matthew...
I dared to buy you
a Book for Christmas).

Merry 2008
♡Mamie

ASPIRE HIGHER

ASPIRE HIGHER

Winning On and Off the Court with Determination, Discipline, and Decisions

Avery Johnson

with Roy S. Johnson

Collins

An Imprint of HarperCollinsPublishers

ASPIRE HIGHER. Copyright © 2008 by Avery Johnson and Roy S.
Johnson. All rights reserved. Printed in the United States of America.
No part of this book may be used or reproduced in any manner
whatsoever without written permission except in the case of brief
quotations embodied in critical articles and reviews. For information,
address HarperCollins Publishers, 10 East 53rd Street, New York,
NY 10022.

HarperCollins books may be purchased for educational, business, or
sales promotional use. For information, please write: Special Markets
Department, HarperCollins Publishers, 10 East 53rd Street, New
York, NY 10022.

FIRST EDITION

Designed by Richard Oriolo

Library of Congress Cataloging-in-Publication Data

Johnson, Avery, 1965-
   Aspire higher : winning on and off the court with determination,
discipline, and decisions / Avery Johnson with Roy S. Johnson. — 1st ed.
       p.   cm.
   ISBN 978-0-06-145277-2
   1. Success.   2. Johnson, Avery, 1965-   I. Johnson, Roy, 1944-
II. Title.
   BJ1611.2.J55 2008
   158—dc22

                                                        2007046194

08 09 10 11 12 WBC/RRD 10 9 8 7 6 5 4 3 2 1

To Jim and Inez Johnson, my late parents.
—Thank you both for making a way.

CONTENTS

FOREWORD BY JERRY JONES   ix

INTRODUCTION   xix

ONE: **Determination**   1

TWO: **Discipline**   21

THREE: **Decisions**   39

FOUR: **Through the Storms: My Story**   63

FIVE: **A Strategy for Success: Standards**   107

SIX: **Systems**   127

SEVEN: **Take a Stand**   147

EIGHT: **Savor the Journey**   165

NINE: **You Are Destined to Win**   187

EPILOGUE
TO OUR YOUTH: CHAMPIONS
UNDER CONSTRUCTION   201

ACKNOWLEDGMENTS   211

FOREWORD

DIDN'T MEET AVERY JOHNSON UNTIL HE joined the coaching staff of the Dallas Mavericks in 2004, but I followed the NBA and watched him when he played for the team. Also, Sidney Moncrief—a fellow University of Arkansas alumnus and a former NBA all-star guard—told me about him when he and I visited each other on occasion. So I was well aware of Avery's leadership qualities, both from hearing of him and watching him perform. Some players create a lot of energy on the court or playing field; they have a certain presence. They have a passion and an awareness of everything going on around them. You obviously think of those guys as coaches of the future.

That was certainly Avery Johnson.

He epitomizes the notion of "aspiring higher." He's lived it, and is still doing so as the Mavericks head coach. He still possesses that certain presence, passion, and awareness that made him a great player, which is why I am confident he'll achieve his "higher" goals here in Dallas as the Mavs' coach.

I love the title "Aspire Higher" because it embodies the way everybody tries to live—or should live. Everybody has goals and dreams, and no matter how small or large those dreams might be, they require the kind of determination, discipline, and decision making that Avery Johnson exhibited throughout his life. His story should be an inspiration to anyone aiming higher.

Success is not complicated. To me, the key is visualization. You must have a picture or an image of how you want it to be or where you're going. Long before you climb into the center of the ring, you have to see yourself there. You have to see yourself facing your opponent with confidence and knowing you're prepared to get the knockout. It's too late if you wait until you're climbing through the ropes. It's too late if you haven't created a picture of yourself hitting the winning shot before you take the court. It's too late to see yourself throwing the game-winning touchdown pass if you wait until you're under center to see yourself making the throw.

You've got to have already seen the vision of yourself in that position long before it happens. If you see yourself as that successful career person you want to be, if you're seeing that and have a clear mental picture of it, making the vision become a reality becomes a lot more logical than it would be otherwise.

If you have the vision of playing center field for the New

York Yankees in your teens, it's more likely to become reality. When you're alone in the backyard, start seeing yourself hitting the big shot or making the big defensive play, then start working toward that vision.

The same is true in business and any professional career. If you don't see yourself as a great surgeon—even while you're in medical school—then it'll never become a rational reality. If you do, no one will be surprised when you get there and become that surgeon.

Avery Johnson didn't suddenly think of himself as head coach of the Dallas Mavericks. I get the sense that when it happened it was no surprise to him. He saw himself there for years. I did not simply wake up one morning a month before I bought the Dallas Cowboys in 1989 and decide I wanted to own and run the team. I'd been thinking about it for a very long time.

In fact, when I was twenty-one years old, I hung out in the lobby of a Dallas hotel just for the chance to see Lamar Hunt, Bud Adams, or any of the men who were meeting to discuss the fledgling American Football League. They were two of eight men who were called "The Foolish Club" for trying to create a competitor to the NFL, but they had a vision and they made that vision a reality. I just wanted to look at them because that's what I wanted to be—an owner.

It took me twenty-four more years to get there—twenty-four years to make the vision a reality by buying the Dallas Cowboys.

I had really great coaching throughout my life. My parents were entrepreneurs, small business people in North Little Rock, Arkansas. Pat and Arminta Jones owned a grocery store, so I learned most of what I know through pure osmosis sitting around the table at meals and working in the store. In order to play sports, I always had to put in time at the store. They emphasized having a strong work ethic. My dad was the role model for me thinking big and having some inordinate goals—goals that may not have made sense to anyone who knew me at the time but were perfectly clear to me.

I played on the 1964 national championship football team under head coach Frank Broyles at Arkansas and experienced that it could happen to me as part of a team that *anticipated* winning the national title and went undefeated. But even while in school, I was doing business. I was a salesman: I sold insurance, I sold shoes, all the while going to school and playing football. And I always had a picture that it would lead to financial success. So when success and new financial heights began to happen for me after college, it was not foreign territory because I'd not only worked, but I had envisioned that I would do inordinate things financially.

If you want to achieve financial success, you should be interested in people who've accomplished a lot financially. You should read and study them to learn their journey and discover what inspired them. I also think you should call them up and ask to visit them. That's what I did when I started out in the oil and real estate businesses, and people were amazingly willing to spend time with me and answer my questions.

Now I do that for young people. During his third year with the Cowboys, Emmitt Smith, who would go on to become the NFL's all-time leading rusher, grabbed me after practice one day and said, "Mr. Jones, between our meetings could I come and just sit on your couch in back of your office and just listen to you talk on the telephone? You won't notice me; I'll just sit there and listen to you talk on the phone." Well, it was kind of unusual, but I thought about it and said, why not. He came and did just as he said. He sat in my office without saying anything and listened. I got very comfortable talking on the phone with him there. He was just listening, soaking it up as I was making deals. Now, Emmitt is making deals of his own as a successful real estate developer not long after he retired as a player. I suspect he envisioned himself doing what I do, then took the steps necessary to make that vision real—down to just hearing how I talked on the phone.

Now I've seen some people with high aspirations who, as they reach for their goals, are unwilling to do some of the small and seemingly menial jobs that they may be asked to do along the way. It may be while they're getting their MBA, or while trying to raise money to start their business. Well, the kinds of jobs you may have to do along the way are very valuable to your understanding of what it takes to achieve success. There are a lot of people who think that just because someone's name is on the door that they're automatically making money. That's not always the case, but outsiders are mesmerized by the material things, the big office, the car, the suits. They take those things at face value. That's a crucial mistake. We're all vulnerable to mistakes. People who have not paid the price for success may not be able to overcome those mistakes as easily as someone who understands how they got there. As you go through the years of being second or third or even last in line, the experience becomes a vital part of your foundation.

That's one issue I have with some of today's pro athletes. Certainly, most of them have achieved an economic status they've never been exposed to. Many were raised without the benefit of some of the good things they're now able to enjoy, so now they still have to work to appreciate the value of the kind of dollars they are getting. If they manage their money, they could provide for the ones they love and the ones they're gonna love for the rest of their lives. But that's a hard concept to understand, I know. Sudden success does not offer that kind of foundation.

Football is a unique experience. Let's face it; there's nothing fun about it. Basketball players play pickup games. Baseball players go out and play catch or take batting practice. You never hear a bunch of guys say, "Hey, let's go out and knock the hell out of each other." A lot of times during practices I'd ask myself: What am I doing out here? This hurts! But you get your ultimate gratification by understanding and remembering the pain you went through to have some success, and then applying those memories as you reach for more.

Most successful entrepreneurs have a certain awareness and understanding of what it took to get there and it never leaves them. John Madden likes to tell the story of how he was sitting out by the practice field one day with my oldest son and some paper was blowing out onto the field. He told my son, "I'll bet you $5 that when your dad comes out there he picks up that paper." Of course, I came out onto the field and picked up the paper. You can always tell who owns a business by who picks the paper up. When you're trying to build something, the little things come automatically, and you try to instill that—coach that—into the people you hire or bring to your team. But picking up the paper comes so natural to entrepreneurs.

When I go to games at home and on the road, I talk to the fans. I sign autographs and thank the people for bringing their kids to the game. I don't care if I'm in Chicago or Minnesota or anywhere else, I do the same thing because I instinctively know what the fans—whether they're Cowboy fans or not—mean to us as owners, coaches, and players in the NFL.

If you're in a corporate environment and striving for a higher place, act like an entrepreneur because what you are actually doing is promoting and selling yourself. And the little things still matter; picking up the paper still matters. Knowing which fork to use at business lunches matters. Seeking out what you don't know rather than sitting there not knowing matters. Knowing how to address everyone in the company matters. Knowing how to look substantive and not frivolous matters. You may not have to know all those things today, but knowing them prepares you for something more. For the doctor, it might prepare you to be head of a state or national medical association. For the employee it might prepare you for a leadership role in an employee organization or union. For the executive it might prepare you to make a significant difference for some charitable organization. For the teacher, it might prepare you to be the local school superintendent or to serve on the president's Council of Education. None of these efforts are meant to distract you from your ultimate goals, but as you're segueing to bigger things, those extra efforts will allow you to make a more meaningful contribution. If you're selling the product (you), you have to work to improve the product.

That's what I've seen in Avery Johnson. He's always looking to improve himself, first as a player and now as a coach and as a leader. I particularly want to underline his communication skills. They are possibly the most impressive I've ever witnessed, and I'm not just talking about in sports. Anywhere, his communication skills are among the best I've seen and heard. He communicates with his entire body and his expressions. He has a way that makes you listen to him, makes you watch him. He projects well to the public and to the media, and he projects well to individuals. This is so important—it's critical—for anyone who seeks to lead. When he speaks, people listen. You can't fake it when you get that kind of attention from people. He's got the meat *and* the potatoes. For true leaders, the substance has to be there. He clearly has a philosophy about how he wants the Mavericks to perform and he's already demonstrated that he certainly has the ability to get other people to do what he wants them to do.

At the end of the day, management—of your career, your organization, your classroom, your team, or your life—comes down to what you can get other people to do. If you can get them to collectively come together and go in a direction that meets the team's goals, you've accomplished the challenge. That's what Avery's best at. His time here in Dallas has been relatively short (so far) but it's been obvious since he arrived that he's able to get people to do what he wants them to do. That's the bottom line: That's a winner.

—Jerry Jones

"I just have faith in myself and in whatever God wants to happen. But I'm going to do my best. If I do my best, He'll do the rest."

INTRODUCTION

IT WASN'T SUPPOSED TO BE ME. Not even six-feet tall, coming from Southern University in New Orleans, and not drafted by a single NBA team. I wasn't supposed to be the guy who played sixteen seasons and won a championship. And, considering all the criticism of my shooting from when I played at St. Augustine High School through the last day of my NBA career, Lord knows I wasn't supposed to be the guy who hit the championship-winning shot in the NBA Finals.

It just wasn't supposed to be me. I wasn't supposed to be an NBA head coach, let alone Coach of the Year, and I wasn't supposed to have an opportunity to coach one of the game's best teams, the Dallas Mavericks, or to coach one of the best players in the world, Dirk Nowitzki.

It wasn't supposed to be me, but it was. It is.

And my journey—from New Orleans' Sixth Ward to the NBA, on the court and on the bench—is a story I need to tell. It's the story of a rise from a place where little was expected of African-American men to being a Black man trying to be a living example of what anyone can do with the right tools, faith, and a strategy. It is the story of someone who began at the bottom and now tries to lift and motivate others to aspire to new heights of their own.

Mine is the story of someone whose faith in God, work ethic, spirit, and passion to overcome obstacles, setbacks, and low expectations can be a blueprint for anyone with high aspirations. Anyone with big dreams.

I want you to aspire higher because I want you to have what I have. I want you to live what I live. I want you to grasp your own dreams in your own way. And I want you to do it despite the odds against you, despite the naysayers around you and despite the challenges and setbacks that will inevitably arise.

I've learned so much along the way. And I've learned from so many. I'm still learning. What I know now is that almost anything is achievable for those willing to nourish their personal gifts with determination, discipline, and sound decision making. What I know is that those tools and a sound strategy are an indomitable arsenal.

My passion and my prayer is to see every student, every schoolteacher, every homemaker, every truck driver, every entrepreneur, every salesperson, every CEO, every husband and wife, every doctor, every social worker, every artist, every dancer, every entertainer, every attorney—everyone—aspire higher. My hope is that my journey will inspire and motivate you and fill you with the courage to reach for your dreams; and that the tools and strategy I offer in these pages will become your own.

Now, hear me on this: I'm not perfect. Not at all. I wasn't a perfect player and I'm not a perfect coach. I'm not a perfect father, nor a perfect husband. Perfection is a worthy goal, though none of us will ever achieve it. That's okay. We can all fall short of perfection and still achieve greatness. As a player, I was part of a team, the San Antonio Spurs, that did just that. We won the 1999 NBA title by beating the New York Knicks in the Finals four games to one. I hit what turned out to be the championship-winning jumper from the left corner with forty-two seconds remaining at Madison Square Garden. A couple of possessions later, the Spurs were NBA champions for the first time in franchise history. Anyone who followed my playing career knows that shooting was my biggest weakness, but I was smart. I studied film. I knew how to learn, and I knew how to win. But you can't always rely on your strengths; sometimes—most of the time, especially if you aspire higher—you also have to strengthen your weaknesses.

That shot was the result of preparation. It was the by-product of a plan that put me in position to take and make that shot. I was prepared to take that shot because I had done the things necessary to be ready. I had been determined to become at least a decent shooter, disciplined in how I approached getting better, and I made smart decisions about when and from where I would shoot.

Determination. Discipline. Decisions. They're the essential tools of success. They are triplets. Peas in a pod. Without any one of them, you are destined to fall short of your goal. I still could have missed that shot, but I would not have been ready to even take the shot had I not been determined, had I not been disciplined to take thousands of shots by myself or with a teammate, and had I not made the decision to commit to becoming a better shooter. I also give a little credit to a teammate who was not even on the floor at the time, Steve Kerr. He'd been a member of three Chicago Bulls championship teams, including one in 1997 (when he buried the game-winning jumper in game six against the Utah Jazz). When he joined the Spurs prior to the 1998–99 season, the first thing I asked him after I welcomed him to the team was, "Steve, how'd you feel when you made that big shot against Utah?" He said, "AJ, the only thing you gotta do is know that you can make it, especially when it's your shot and you get the opportunity. You just gotta relish it and just salivate over it and just step up and knock it down."

Talk about a recipe for success: You just *gotta know* you can achieve your goal, and when opportunity arises you have to *relish* it, *salivate* over it, and just *step up and knock it down.* Just thinking about those words gets me excited.

I was not supposed to be the guy to take the shot, but I stepped up and knocked it down.

I was also not supposed to be Coach of the Year and lead the

Mavericks to the 2005–06 NBA Finals in my second season, but I had been preparing to coach for almost as long as I can remember. I didn't know where I was going to coach, or what, or even if it would be in sports, but my late father used to always say I was going to coach something because I "talked so much." Of course we lost that series against Shaquille O'Neal, Dwyane Wade, and the Miami Heat, four games to two. We lost four straight after taking a two-games-to-none lead. It was devastating for us all. After the last game, none of us wanted to leave the locker room. There was silence. There was nothing. Higher aspirations, as close as they may appear to be, do not always come to fruition, but those experiences are part of the necessary steps you will take along the way as you aspire higher. And the setbacks can be more valuable than the successes. Don't I know.

In 2006–07, we almost achieved historic greatness. We won sixty-seven games and were the best team in the league for nearly the entire regular season. Though we didn't talk about it, the seventy-win mark, which had been achieved by only one NBA team throughout the league's history—the 1995–96 Bulls—may have crept into our minds. It was a tantalizing nugget but the record was never our goal. Winning the title was. Losing to the Golden State Warriors in the first round of the playoffs was painful, but no more so than if we'd lost in a later round.

Losing is losing. The Warriors had not reached the postseason in thirteen years, and didn't earn their playoff berth until the final day of the season, but give them credit. They played brilliantly. They played with heart and passion. Their leader, point guard Baron Davis, played like an alien, he was out of this world.

Despite the pain, a real positive came out of that experience. It actually hit me as I began working on this book. Aspiring higher isn't just something I want for *you*, it's actually where *I* am in my career, too. I haven't won my championship as a coach. We haven't won our championship as a team. I'm exactly where you are. I'm in between.

Being born is easy. So is taking your last breath. Everything in between, that's the hard part. Life is in-between, and it will offer challenges and opportunities beyond measure.

I'm where my coauthor, Roy S. Johnson, is as he aspires higher in his career as a journalist, television sports commentator, and media consultant. In between.

I'm where the young entrepreneur is as she aspires to start her business. In between.

I'm where the teacher is as he tries to pull more out of his students. In between.

I'm where the truck driver is as he tries to earn more for his family. In between.

I'm where the new CEO is as she tries to inspire her employees, raise the stock price, and deliver better value to shareholders. I'm right where anyone is who's trying to aspire higher. We are all in between

I'm right where you are—in between.

This book offers the lessons I've learned and the strategies

I've used—and am still using—to become a better coach, a better husband and father, a better man.

Aspiring higher begins with a self-assessment, which can be painful. You really have to take an honest look not just at yourself. You must then look at the people around you. If those around you don't share your vision, it is difficult to accomplish your goals—particularly if you work closely with them. Last summer, following our loss to Golden State, I had to step outside of myself and take a hard look both at myself and the team and ask, Do I *really* want to aspire higher? What the question really should be is: Do I want to make the *commitment* to aspire higher? Once I determined that the answer was "yes," then it was time to create and implement the plan.

The first section of the book takes a "big picture" look at the characteristics, the tools, required to aspire higher. I've mentioned them before: Determination, Discipline, and Decisions. Those chapters outline the importance of those simple traits for anyone with high aspirations. They are the foundation for success. Any successful person will tell you that they would not have achieved anything without making a commitment to those three traits.

If the first section of the book provides the tools, the last section outlines the strategy for aspiring higher, my "S Plan": Standards, System, Stand, and Savor. It's been the foundation of my efforts to transform the Mavericks from an offensive team known only for lighting up the scoreboard to a defensive-minded team capable of competing for a championship. Defense is how you win in our league. Defense and being able to score against any opposition and under pressure is how you win. Winning—in the NBA and in life—is based on being able to impose your will onto whatever challenge stands in your path: your opponent, your competition, your lack of experience, your lack of confidence, your talent, anything. And to do that you must be committed to a sound and solid strategy.

It starts with setting the highest *standards* for personal achievement. The Mavericks had never come close to winning an NBA title before I became head coach in 2004, so my mission began with making it clear to my players that winning an NBA title was the goal. It was the new standard. Being satisfied with anything less was out of the question. "It all starts with high goals," I told them. "So you must ask, 'What are my goals? What am I reaching for?'" Set your standards high.

Now you must give yourself the best opportunity to reach those new standards, so you'll need a *system* designed to do that. You'll need to design the steps necessary to meet the standards. If the new standards are a change in your behavior you might need to eliminate some bad influences from your life. Without a system designed to put you in position to meet your standards, those standards may not be worth a leftover timeout.

Next, at some point on your path you'll be asked to make a critical decision—one that will require you to take a *stand*. You will have to know what is acceptable and what is not—and you must tolerate nothing less. I asked my players to search inside themselves to determine what they stood for individually, and how they want to be characterized as a team. How do *you* want to be known? This is a matter of ethics, integrity, and spiritual-ity. How do you want to be characterized en route to your goals?

Then you must commit to living the life you want to stand for—every day, every hour, every moment. In 1989, in the sum-mer following my rookie NBA season in Seattle, I was forced to decide for myself what I stood for and whether I was willing to live by the standards I set. At the time I did not like the person I'd become. This crossroad I came to actually occurred on the Mississippi River Bridge crossing from downtown New Orleans to the west bank. And right there on the bridge I chose my path and committed to living a faith-based life. I took a stand and committed completely.

Finally, and perhaps most importantly, you must, must, must *savor* the journey. Savor every moment of the challenge. Savor the process. Savor the steps. Even savor the setbacks. For the Mavs it isn't simply the great play or the great defensive stand we savor, it's the hundreds of times we ran the play or drilled the defense in practice. Savor it all.

Once you have established high standards, created systems for achieving those standards, taken a stand for what you believe in, and started to savor the process of aspiring higher, you will be on your way. You'll have put yourself in position to achieve what you set out to do, and you'll have done it in a way that re-flects your best *you*.

Along the way in this book I'll share a bit of my life's journey. I'll share with you the men and women who inspired me along the way, the challenges I've overcome, and the highs and lows that make up my story. It's a long way from the housing projects of New Orleans to a head coach's seat in the NBA, but it is not longer, nor more fulfilling, than the path you can take as well. My experiences as an athlete, coach, father, husband, brother, teacher, friend, and leader will help you to aspire higher.

ONE

Determination

DETERMINATION MEANS REFUSING TO TAKE NO for an answer. It means refusing to be rejected. I'm not talking about being stubborn in a negative way; determination means being stubborn in a good way. You are still teachable, you listen to reason. You are always looking to learn, always hungry to get better. You're determined, but not a jerk.

You are determined to let nothing stand in the way of achieving your goal. You are determined to be honest with yourself about choosing the right goal and sticking with it. Whether that goal is to get a new job, change your career, become the CEO, or simply excel at your current job, determination is the first key.

Stubbornness—positive stubbornness, that is—can take you places you never thought you could go. It can make you do things you thought you never could do. Determination stretches you, it makes more of you than was there before. It stretches your mental capacities. It challenges you.

In 1982, at the beginning of my senior year at St. Augustine High School, my friend Derrick Lafayette and I didn't want to take the math class that was assigned to us. We wanted to take the higher math class with the gifted students, a trigonometry class taught by Dr. Carl A. Blouin. The administrators told us we couldn't do it. Because we were athletes, they figured we weren't smart enough.

But we were determined. So we jumped through hoops to get into that class. We petitioned the math department; we had our parents call the teachers; we refused to take no for an answer; we did everything we could to get into this math class. We were *determined* to get in. Finally the administration let us in. Our determination inspired us to be undeterred by those who had lower expectations for us than we had for ourselves.

Now, what we didn't know was the level of determination needed just to get a C! The other kids in the class didn't need determination. They were just gifted. They didn't have to work as hard. During the first two quarters, we both earned Fs and Ds, but we didn't give up. We decided to do something about it. We went to nearby Xavier University to find tutors. To pay for them, we washed cars on the weekend. We would drive over to each other's houses late at night for extra studying. We were *determined* to pass that class. We worked harder than we knew we could and ended up with Bs in the third and fourth quarters to pull our overall grade to a C. That's the best C I ever made in my life.

Most people didn't think I was big enough, strong enough, or good enough to play in the NBA. Through determination, I proved all those people wrong. Determination can keep you on the right path, despite the odds against you and any shortcomings you might have. For example, in 1991, three years into my NBA career as a player, I was cut by the Denver Nuggets. A lot of people told me to retire, to quit. My wife even told me to quit—probably because she was pregnant and we were broke—but I said no because I knew that despite my size and my background playing for a small Black college, I was gifted enough to play in the NBA and I was determined to prove myself right and others wrong.

That's why it's important to always play, study, and pursue your craft with determination. There's a premium for playing with passion. Don't be discouraged by a setback—any setback. Even after I was released I knew I was going to make it back. How? Determination.

But hear me on this: Determination shouldn't be blind; it needs to be focused. The first step is to *determine* your goals, based on a truthful self-assessment of your own passions and skills. What do you enjoy doing? Are you good enough to succeed on the path you've chosen? Your goals should not only be based on what you see and hear, they must come from your heart and your head. You need to be on a path that you love and you need to have the skills to reach your destination. We can all be swayed by what we perceive to be the benefits of certain professions: money and celebrity. Those factors can push you onto a path that's not right for you. There's no sense trying to become a singer or rapper if you can't carry a tune or rhyme. There's no sense in aspiring to be a doctor if you're not truly interested in helping people. Or you can end up on a career path where you're simply not good enough to succeed at the professional level. Sure, you might love to play basketball but if you don't love the sport, that path isn't right for you.

Let's be real here. There are some guys who are determined to play in the NBA, but who simply aren't good enough. They need to sell cars or teach; do the thing they're gifted in. They're just not gifted enough at basketball to play in the NBA. I had a player in training camp recently who was one of the most timid guys I've ever seen in my life, but he was smart. He was an absolute whiz at math. He understood the ins and outs of the stock market. After long conversations with this guy, I knew he needed to be on Wall Street, not in the NBA. Basketball was not his gift. He needed to go start a hedge fund or some kind of private equity firm.

He had determination, but it was the wrong determination. Basketball wasn't his gift—numbers were.

Sometimes our determination is framed by others, by what others think we should be doing or by what we see on television or on the Internet. One of the challenges we all have is being true to ourselves and mindful of our real gifts. Too many people want prosperity, but they're unable to focus on whether they have what it takes to get there. If you're honest with yourself, you become determined to choose the right path and stay on it.

My father didn't tell me that I was going to be a basketball player. He didn't tell me that at all but he saw my true talent from an early age. I mentioned in the Introduction that he knew I was going to be a coach because I loved to talk. What he actually said was, "Listen, I don't know what you're going to be. You may be a doctor; you may end up running your own company; you may be called to be a preacher; you may be a coach; you may be a CEO. I don't know where you'll end up but it's going to be somewhere you can talk. You can persuade people. You can lead." He said those things because he really loved me, he wasn't trying to make money off me, and he wasn't just telling me what I wanted to hear. Right away, he saw my ability to help push others to the peak of their own abilities.

You also have to know when to change the path you're on. During my third stint with the Spurs, I played for two different coaches, Bob Hill and Gregg Popovich, who we all called Pop. Sometimes during practice they would turn to me and say, "Coach, what do you want to do today?"

Now remember, this was when I was still a player. I'd just look at them and laugh but they wouldn't stop. They insisted they wanted my ideas for practice that day. Pop would say, only half kidding: "No, you are the coach. I work for you."

The point is that even though you need to stay determined to achieve the goals you've chosen, no matter what other people think, you can also benefit by listening to the people around you. Whether by design—or divine—or not, they might be telling you exactly what you need to hear regarding your gifts. When I was young, I heard it from my dad. When I was older, I heard it from Bob Hill and Pop. I was meant to be a coach. Because I had those types of people around me, shaping me and molding me and giving me confidence, I was very clear about what I wanted to do with my life—as Jack Nicholson said in *A Few Good Men*, I was "crystal clear" about the direction of my life. So everything I am doing now, from coaching to teaching to speaking to groups of all sizes—even writing this book—is by design. I've been determined to succeed at it.

Who do you listen to? One of your challenges is to figure out who truly has your best interests in mind. I heard a guy talk about this in church one Sunday in a service aimed at men. He said,

> Determination comes from the word *determine*. Men, you've got to know how to determine the right type of man to listen to. Your ears hear many voices. You have to determine which voices are speaking life and which are speaking death. Who do you surround yourself with? The inner circle of men—and, yes, women—who speak to you in your life is critical in determining whether you achieve your dreams. What type of men are going to help you win?

The way I win is to surround myself with the right type of friends, men and women who, at crunch time, will not judge me or abandon me. Neglecting to surround yourself with winners is like kryptonite to your determination. So many of our stars—from business leaders to entertainers to athletes—have fallen not because they weren't determined but because they surrounded themselves with losers and manipulators. Too often, the advice offered by certain people in our lives becomes a death trap that leads to bitterness, depression, and anger. You might be encouraged by a so-called friend to be jealous of a colleague or to shirk some responsibilities and go party instead. That's not going to help you aspire higher. That only helps you lose.

There are also people who try to aspire higher through you. They think you are their ticket to the big time, their road to riches. One of the many things I loved about my mother and father is that they didn't feel I had to rescue them from poverty. They didn't push me to play in the NBA. They pushed me to develop my gift. They pushed me to always be determined at whatever I decided to do.

Too often manipulators and losers will try to push you toward something that is not your gift. It's really *their* gift, their free gift that they're looking to receive through you. They might encourage you not because they love you but merely for the benefits to them. If the heart of the advisor, or your so-called friend, is not to help you aspire higher they must be eliminated from your circle. We'll talk more about what to do in that situation in Chapter 3, Decisions.

I've been blessed to have been surrounded, nurtured, and encouraged by the right type of men. From Ben Jobe, my coach at Southern; to Pop at Golden State and in San Antonio; to Don Nelson (or "Nellie") at Golden State and in Dallas; to the owner of the Dallas Mavericks Mark Cuban; our team chaplin, Pastor Tony Evans; and, of course, my dad, Jim Johnson: They are the right type of men. This is nothing against women. There have been strong important women in my life, too. And there are many women—single mothers—who play both roles well. But even they will admit that young men need the right type of men in their lives. I had those men. They encouraged me and stretched my gifts. They helped me win.

Determination can also take you in a negative direction if your motivation is not properly aligned. One of the most determined individuals I ever played with was Dennis Rodman. Dennis was determined, but his determination was all about himself, his stats, his role on the team. Basketball fans know him as a relentless rebounder who was part of the "Bad Boy" Detroit Pistons championship teams. He was my teammate on the San Antonio Spurs during the 1994–95 season. Led by David Robinson, who was at the peak of his career, we had a very good regular season and finished up 60–22. In fact, that was the best team I ever played for or coached—the most talented team. We started the season losing eleven of our first twenty games. Do the math and you'll see how good we were by the playoffs. Vinny Del Negro and I were the backcourt, Sean Elliott at small forward, Rodman at power forward, and Robinson in the middle. Our backups were guards Doc Rivers and Willie Anderson; forwards Chuck Person, Terry Cummings, and "the cheerleader" Jack Haley; with J.R. Reid and a fellow named Moses Malone backing up at center. We were *physical*. Rodman was our leading rebounder, averaging almost seventeen boards a game. That's astonishing. Unfortunately, Rodman was also our leading distraction. He didn't act like part of the team. He was late to games. He missed practices. Everyone saw him taking off his shoes on the sideline.

We reached the Western Conference finals but lost to Hakeem Olajuwon and the Houston Rockets, who went on to win the title. Quite simply, he was the best player on the floor and they were the better team in that series. After the season we all knew we weren't going to achieve our goal of winning a title with Rodman, despite his numbers. He was the polar opposite of our leader, David Robinson, and it was a negative for our team. Opposite personalities can be beneficial but instead of complementing and inspiring David, Dennis irritated him. You don't win with an irritated leader. Dennis was the opposite of everything David represented. They had no communication. David, as our captain, tried to get through to Dennis, but he couldn't. Dennis had no respect for David. He was a "bad boy," period. David Robinson was a good man, and he was not going to compromise his integrity to be more likable to Dennis. At the end of the season, Dennis was traded to the Chicago Bulls. A few years later we won our title without him. Sure, Dennis won a title the following season with the Chicago Bulls, but I only need two words to explain that: Michael Jordan.

Fortunately, I've had the pleasure of playing with and coaching many players who showed the right kind of determination. Two of the most determined players I've seen are Tim Duncan and Dirk Nowitzki. If I were to pick three words to describe those guys I'd say determined, determined, and determined. Am I being clear enough? Tim doesn't talk much, not like me, but he's determined just the same. I noticed it the day that I met him, on the first day of training camp during his rookie season when I saw him outplay everybody, including David Robinson.

That night, I was so excited. I couldn't sleep. I thought to myself, "This is not real." He was Karl Malone and Hakeem all rolled into one. He had the footwork, the power, the moves. He could run and block shots. But it was the determination that really made him special—makes him special.

Tim had had a great college career at Wake Forest University. He was smooth, polished, and effective. Possibly the only other post man with footwork as good was Hakeem. Tim stayed in college four years, which was unusual even back then for someone with so much talent. Typically, guys who stay in school that long are perceived by NBA folks as having peaked; it is assumed that they won't get any better in the NBA. Not Tim. He went to another level, almost immediately, and against better talent. Now he is among the best big men ever. Most guys can't make that adjustment. He was a star in college and because of his determination to continue to improve he became a superstar in the pros.

I'll never forget Mario Elie and me telling Tim during the 1998–99 finals, when he helped the Spurs win their first championship: "If you've got single coverage, score the ball; double coverage, score the ball; triple coverage, pass." We just kept telling him: "You lead us home." He did, and I think the reinforcement we gave him helped develop the determination he still shows today.

Dirk is determined in a different way. No one I've played with or coached works as hard on his game. His preparation is unmatched. He was determined not to be just another international statistic—a player known for being able to score but not win. He was determined to be a superstar, which he is. Before and after every practice, Dirk shoots and trains and shoots and trains and shoots and trains. Even before games, he's at it. He's now double- and sometimes triple-teamed and he still finds ways to succeed at an all-star level. He has not won an NBA championship like Tim—not yet anyway. But he's just as determined.

Patrick Ewing was another guy who was determined. He aspired to be a champion. While aspiring higher doesn't always result in the affirmation of success, the lesson derived from the effort may be fulfilling itself, and can be even more valuable than achieving the original goal. He led his teams to the finals twice and retired from the game known as one of its best leaders and most determined players. Even though he never reached his goal of winning an NBA championship, his journey was still a success by any measure. We can all learn from that.

It's easy to maintain your determination when things are going well, but can you sustain it in the face of a challenge? The pastor can easily maintain his fire at the peak of his sermon when the congregation is showering him with hallelujahs, but can he muster it later in the week when a member comes to him with a tragedy? The CEO is all smiles when his stock is on the rise but how about when the value falls and he's facing a room full of angry shareholders? Mom and Dad are proud of their parenting skills when their kids are doing well in school and are singing in the church choir, but what happens when the teacher calls with news that their kids' grades are falling and they're being disruptive in class? Those are the times when you need your determination most of all if you're committed to aspiring higher.

Your own determination will be challenged at various times in your life. There will be some point when you are not as successful as you've been in the past. Your grades might slip, your sales numbers might taper off, your profits might decline. That's when you have to stay determined or else you may become distracted and lose connection with reality.

The difficulty for a lot of great players comes on the downside of their careers when suddenly their skills start to erode and all the determination in the world won't bring them back. It was difficult for me at the end of my playing career.

In basketball, every player must face the reality that they can't play forever. As a coach, when you see a player who's at the end of his career you just want to tell them, "It's over for you, man." You know they can't see it when their skills deteriorate and it's not a pretty sight. Other players start to distance themselves. Even still, some guys still try to keep going. Maybe they take a year or two off and then come back and play. You want to tell them, "Come on, man. It just doesn't work like that."

When you reach one of those crossroads, you have to have an honest conversation with yourself. You don't want your determination to become clouded by misinformation. Fortunately, in most professions, our skills stay sharp much longer than they do on the basketball court. Your new lack of effectiveness may be due to a number of factors. Don't let challenges cloud your reality. Instead, use them as an opportunity to reassess it and reaffirm your determination. Break down your problems and tackle them head on, with the help of your trusted inner circle. Don't "lose weight"—stay F.A.T: faithful, available, and teachable.

Before I retired as a player, I'd always told myself that I wanted to go out feeling good. But because I refused to have a conversation with reality, because I did not listen to the men I had put around me, for a time there my determination was hurting me, *not* helping me. I was determined in such a way that I didn't care what anybody said, what anybody thought, or what was written in the local papers.

Finally, God put a young man in my life that delivered a strong message about my new reality. His name was Devin Harris. He was Dallas' first-round draft pick in 2004, a quick point guard from Wisconsin. I finished the 2003–04 season, my sixteenth, with Golden State. It had been a rough year. We weren't very good and I missed my family back in Houston. After the season I was contemplating retirement—not the first time I'd done so, mind you—when Mark Cuban and Don Nelson brought me back to Dallas as a player/coach—but at training camp, in practices and scrimmages, Devin quickly let me know that it was over. He ran by me like I was a streetlight and when he guarded me my body simply could not do what my brain wanted it to do. My brain was determined, but my body was not able to deliver. After a couple of ankle-breaking, knee-bending crossovers, I finally told Cuban I didn't want to play anymore and Nellie made me his top assistant. Devin Harris introduced me to my new reality and permanently retired me. That's why I still fuss at him every day.

When I look back at the path of my own career and the men who were around me, I see clearly that the path chosen for me was coaching. Playing was great. The experiences it provided were memorable and it was certainly lucrative, but I realize now that it was all preparing me to coach. My first years struggling with Seattle and Denver prepared me to deal with the players at the end of the bench, and players whose determination to play clouded the reality that they simply weren't good enough. The men I met along the way prepared me to learn how to manage, and my successes prepared me to teach men and women how to win.

Now, I believe I can coach in any capacity. That's not an arrogant statement. I can coach athletes, salesmen, teachers, or CEOs because it's all coaching. It's all management.

It's about being a master manager. Other people can teach the skills, to field the ball, hit the ball, and catch the ball, but it's hard to teach, or to coach, determination. It's hard to coach people to stretch themselves to aspire higher. That is the crux of being a master manager.

How do you learn determination? You begin by considering your environment—your work environment, your spiritual environment, your nutritional environment, your relationship and family environments. Why? Because your environment shapes your determination.

It's hard to be determined when you come from an abusive home. It's hard to be determined when you come from a school with out-of-date books and teachers who are afraid of their students. It's hard to be determined without the support of your spouse or your manager or your teammates. It's hard to be determined when you confront challenges or setbacks—when your grades slip, when your profits decline, when your friends are critical. It's hard to be determined in a "me" environment, where selfishness overwhelms selflessness.

As difficult as it may be, if you find yourself in a negative, nonsupportive environment, do your best to not allow it to affect your self-esteem, to diminish how you think of yourself. Don't allow the environment to poison your principles, preparation, perseverance, or your pursuit of happiness. Don't let it poison your personality. Turn the poison into a positive by being just a little bit selfish about yourself. In a negative environment, it's okay to be a bit selfish. In a negative environment, it's okay to have a "me" attitude. It's okay not to put others first or to not be concerned about how others think of you. Put your blinders on, tune them out, and focus on your goals.

This is the time to think about your relationship with you. It's the time to be sensitive to your own feelings, to no one but yourself. Sometimes your friends aren't your friends. Everybody that's kin to you is not necessarily "kin" to you. Just because they have the same blood doesn't mean they have the same spirit. You've got to limit the amount of contact you have with those people who poison your environment. I read in another book that it takes five positive remarks to counter the effects of one negative remark. It increases tenfold if the negative remark is made between spouses or people especially close to you.

How you handle a poisonous environment will affect your ability to aspire higher. It will interrupt your determination. Remember watching television as a child, when your program would get interrupted by the test pattern and the ominous voice said: "This is a test of the emergency broadcast system." At the end the voice would say: "This was only a test." Likewise, poisonous environments are *only a test*. But they can be worse—poison can kill you, remember—if you allow them to interrupt your determination.

What you see will implant itself in your mind. The images will get into your heart, where they inspire your confidence and fuel your determination. Determined people are confident people, and their confidence is influenced by what they've seen.

When I was young I saw small guards like Nate "Tiny" Archibald, Isiah Thomas, and Tyrone "Mugsy" Bogues succeed in the NBA, and it gave me confidence that I could succeed, too. Even when I was the last man on the bench and not playing at all in high school at St. Augustine or in college, I kept my confidence by holding onto the images of Tiny, Isiah, and Mugsy. I knew what it meant to be a good father and husband because my own father was a good example for me. Knowing someone who graduated from college helped me to understand that I could do it, too.

When I heard people say that I was good enough to graduate from college, to be a great leader, a great coach, or minister to people, it inspired me to begin visualizing myself doing all of those things. Once I began seeing myself accomplishing those things they became more real, more concrete. They took root in my heart, which made my confidence grow and empowered me. You need to do the same things with your goals—especially if you're stuck in a negative environment. Tune out the naysayers, look inside yourself, and find people who will support you— they're out there somewhere.

Often, winners are not necessarily the most talented competitors. It's not always about talent. It's about heart. Having confidence in your heart strengthens you. It gives you courage to exceed the limitations others may have placed on you, or that you may have placed on yourself. You need confidence to overcome those limitations and meet the challenges that will inevitably arise and threaten to diminish your determination.

Things will happen over which you have no control. Injuries and accidents happen. Mistakes happen. In basketball, turnovers and missed shots happen. But they can be overcome—with heart. Sports fans—coaches, too–often talk about athletes who don't have a lot of talent but who succeed anyway. They have a lot of heart. The Bible in James 2:20 says, "...faith without works is dead." You can be talented, but without confidence and heart, you will not be able to overcome the person who just may be more talented than you, or to face the challenges and obstacles that will arise.

The Bible also says, in Romans 2:11, "there is no respect of persons with God," meaning you should never think others can be blessed with "talents," as your personal gifts are called in the Bible, and that you cannot be blessed. Envying the success of others is no way to aspire higher. It only serves to distract and diminish your own determination. Instead, use others' successes as inspiration. Believe that if they can do it, so can you, in your own way. You can be great with whatever your gifts may be. Maybe you won't be a millionaire lawyer or doctor or entrepreneur like your friend or someone you know, but you must believe that your gift is the perfect one for you.

Boost your confidence by embracing the images of others who have succeeded before you. For me it was Tiny, Isiah, and Mugsy. As a coach, I was inspired by K. C. Jones and Lenny Wilkens—two men who looked like me, African-American men—winning NBA championships as coaches. One day, I am sure a young Black coach will tell you how they were inspired by Indianapolis coach Tony Dungy's victory in Super Bowl XXIX over the Chicago Bears, who were coached by another African-American man, Lovie Smith. Who are the heroes in your industry? Who are the success stories who overcame the kinds of odds you face in your own effort to aspire higher?

In 2006, the year we went to the NBA Finals, I'd been telling my guys all season long that they were the best team in the NBA, but they didn't believe me until we actually *reached* the Finals. All year long I tried to give them confidence. That's something that every good manager needs to try to pass along to his or her employees. Help them find roles in which they feel confident.

As a player, I was very confident from the left corner at about sixteen feet. It was like I owned that small piece of property. It doesn't make any sense. Sixteen feet is sixteen feet, isn't it? If I'm confident from that distance I should be confident anywhere on the floor. I wasn't. But put me in that left corner right now and I'll go out there and make ten in a row. That's what I believe in my heart because at some time in my career, I saw it—I hit several shots from that spot and that planted it in my mind. Confidence.

How did Michael Jordan come through in crunch time every time? Sure he was talented, but he was also determined and he had confidence. It all happened because confidence was in his heart, because it was in his mind. He was mentally tough, and he visualized success; that couldn't be shaken by anything or anybody, on or off the court. That's confidence.

Confidence allows you to begin your ascent. It starts with what you see, what you hear, what you visualize, and finally what you place in your heart. A lot of times my wife will tell me, "Baby, keep your money. Just give me your heart. I'd rather have your heart." Money comes and goes; the heart is forever.

When I was with the Spurs, I used to get really, really angry with Pop, but he had my heart. We had some heated exchanges through the years—mainly over strategy. Pop had a certain way he wanted to do things, mainly on defense. I'd disagree. Most of the time I gave in. I respected him as a coach and as an authority figure. He always thought I was the worst defender and I thought I wasn't as bad as he thought I was. Of course he thought everybody was awful on defense. There were so many halftimes in San Antonio when all it seemed he talked about was how bad a defender I was. Not only me, though, everybody. David got it. Tim got it. The worst part was that I used to come home and complain about Pop to my wife and she'd say, "He's right." Now that would hurt.

But he had my heart. He was one of the first basketball people to see past my weaknesses and embrace me for my strengths. When other coaches said I could never succeed because I was not a great shooter, he saw my leadership abilities. He saw my toughness. He saw my communication skills.

Throughout my career, he was my angel, someone who I knew always had my best interests at heart. That's why he had *my* heart. Pop called me several times during my playing career to say, "Pack your bags," because I was either being traded to another team or being offered the opportunity to sign with him and his team. Whatever the situation, I knew it was going to be for the better because I knew Pop wanted only the best for me. That's why he had my heart.

Determination begins with the heart, and it is the beginning of success.

Discipline

ACTIVATING YOUR GIFT REQUIRES DISCIPLINE. Developing your talent requires discipline. Discipline causes you to discover what you must do, every day, in order to fulfill your dream. It's what gets you to the office fifteen minutes before everyone else each day, or to the gym every morning at 6:00 a.m. It's what causes Venus Williams to hit five hundred forehands every day. What is it that motivated Bill Gates and Paul Allen to try and try and try again until they created their first computer? Discipline.

Discipline makes that daily duty that you simply must perform more important than almost anything else. Nobody has to force you to read that extra textbook. No one has to force you to rewrite those lyrics just one more time. You don't need to be reminded or pushed to do it. To you, it's not optional. It's something you have to do, and that action, inspired by discipline, increases your potential to aspire higher.

A good friend of mine describes discipline as a safeguard. He once said to me, "What I do in my life is put up safeguards to protect myself. There are certain barriers I put up around myself that help keep me disciplined." I always thought that was a great description. A boxer can only fight inside the ring. The ropes are there to keep him contained. If he gets outside the ropes, there are consequences and penalties; he loses control. If he gets outside the ropes, the fight is stopped. In our lives, discipline is like those ropes. It surrounds us and helps us make the right decisions to achieve the goals we have determined.

When our team goes to certain cities—Miami, Atlanta, and New York—we install a safeguard in order to ensure that we stay disciplined: a curfew. The reason should be obvious. Those are the cities with the most distractions for our young players. For us, playing on the road isn't travel for pleasure, it's a business trip. Our goal is to win an NBA championship. If we're going to achieve that goal, we have to stay disciplined, continue to improve, and prepare ourselves for the postseason. We can't do that if our players have been out too late, and that's why we have the curfew as a safeguard. Not that we don't allow our players to have fun. Fun and parties have their place in life, but our coaches talk to the players about knowing when to party. When it's time to party, I'm right there with them. When it's time to go to work, we have to all be on the same page.

If you're a young ballplayer and you want to become a better shooter, you've got to have the discipline to consistently get up every morning and go shoot five hundred shots. You're not going to be able to do that if you've been out partying at the wrong time. You've got to have the discipline to take those five hundred shots every day. Other people in your life are going to try to distract you from that. They don't mean any harm by it, but that's what they'll do. You have to stay disciplined and resist that temptation. When they tempt you with something that sounds like more fun than shooting those five hundred shots, you've got to have the discipline to turn them down.

That's how determination and discipline work together. The goal that you've determined is to become a better shooter. The discipline is committing to taking those shots no matter what distractions may present themselves.

Of course this works in other areas of life as well. Let's say you want to graduate from college. That is the goal you have determined. The question is, do you have the discipline to study when everybody else is out partying? Maybe you want to be an entrepreneur. You're able to come up with a creative idea and you're willing to put in the work, but do you have the discipline to forgo certain social activities, like movies and eating out, so you can save the necessary money to get your business off the ground? You want to be a preacher but do you have the discipline to attend divinity school and lead the kind of moral life that will cause people to follow where you lead? Or are you just focused on the material benefits of preaching and becoming a small-g "god" in your community? Each of those goals requires determination, but without discipline, those goals are going to be out of reach no matter how badly you want to achieve them.

Here's another way to think of these tenets of success: You are driving toward a specific destination. Determination is the motor; without it, you're not going anywhere. You're not leaving the driveway. You're stuck right where you are. Determination gets you out on the road. What is discipline? The road signs and signals that are put in place in order to help you arrive at your destination safely. "Do Not Enter," or you might drive into on-coming traffic. Obey the "Speed Limit," or you might lose control of the car. Stay within the yellow and white lines on the road, or you may cause an accident. It takes all of those elements in order for you to get where you want to go.

How key is discipline to the journey? Think back to a time in your life when you failed at something. We've all been there, including me. Sometimes the failures are professional—a missed deadline, a job we didn't get. Other times they are personal—an unhealthy romance or a strained relationship with a family member. In most cases, it's not that you weren't determined, it's that you weren't disciplined enough. Maybe you didn't work that extra hour or do that additional research before your interview. Maybe you just couldn't let that comment go unanswered, and you had to continue the fight. Whatever the case, if you were more disciplined, you would have had a much better chance for success.

A lack of discipline can really hurt you in other areas of your life as well, particularly in financial terms. Why does debilitating credit card debt happen? A lack of discipline is usually at fault. At some point you decided you were going to spend more than you make. How do you become overweight? A lack of discipline, again. You decided to eat more calories than you were able to burn. Why did your marriage fail? If you ask most divorced men why their marriage failed, they just say, "Man I was stupid. I was foolish." Well that may be true, but it's also probably true that they lacked the discipline to be good partners. Why have you talked for years about changing careers or starting a business, yet you remain in the same job rut? You may be determined, and you may even know *how* to make the moves, but in the end, you lack the discipline to make it happen.

On the other hand, if you have discipline, there isn't any area of your life that won't improve. One of the things I love to hear when I travel with my kids is when we get off the airplane and other passengers say, "Your children are great. They weren't noisy; they weren't kicking the back of my seat. They weren't throwing food all over. How do you do that?" "Discipline," I say. My wife, Cassandra, and I taught them the proper boundaries of good behavior at an early age.

How? Like that boxer who tries to fight out of the ring, my kids know that there are consequences for acting outside the boundaries of good behavior. There are consequences when they get out of line.

When it comes to these consequences, my wife and I are "old

school." Some people believe in giving their kids a "time-out" when they get out of line. That doesn't always work. I wish my dad had believed in time-outs. I wish the Josephite priests at St. Augustine High School had believed in time-outs. It would have saved my rear end from extremely painful days.

Too many parents these days try to buy their children, rather than instilling discipline by creating boundaries and enforcing consequences for stepping outside those boundaries. They offer rewards for behavior that should be everyday practice, and fail to create real consequences for bad behavior. In the end they're only buying behavior—they're not developing discipline—and that's something that might hurt their children for the rest of their lives.

A big part of teaching kids discipline is instilling a work ethic as soon as possible. When I was a teenager, my dad told me: "You want a car, work for it." My fourteen-year-old daughter looked at me like I was crazy when I told her she'd have to get a job that summer. I explained to her,

> You've got to work. It might be at your favorite store in the mall, but it's got to be somewhere. I'm not trying to punish you; I'm trying to instill the values of discipline in you. What do you want in life? No matter what it is, in this world, no matter who you are, if you don't work you don't eat.

I told my twelve-year-old son that when the time comes, it will be the same thing for him: "In two years, you'll work. It doesn't matter if it's at the pool folding towels or at a doughnut shop, but you're getting a j-o-b. I'm not saying you've got to work eight hours every day; it might be a little, part-time gig, but you're going to do something." He didn't say anything. Maybe he's hoping I'll forget. The bad news for him is that I've got the discipline to remember.

If you're a coach or a manager in a corporation there are different ways to instill discipline in your players or employees. In order to succeed, it is critical to be clear regarding the boundaries for their behavior. It is just as critical to provide the safeguards that allow them to be comfortable within those boundaries. The last step is to have consequences when members of your team step outside the boundaries. In basketball, the consequences are fines, extra running during practice, or simply a cutback in playing time. That is the most effective consequence for an athlete. I can't punish them quite like I do my children, but I can take away something they value, and they value nothing more than playing time. Losing playing time affects them in the short term (just take a look at any disgruntled player on the bench during a game) and the long term (contract time).

Enforcing consequences—whether on your team, your staff, or even on yourself—will cause some short-term pain but is a necessary reminder that achieving any goal will be fraught with challenges. It's going to take time if you want to do it right, and that's where I have a problem with the way a lot of people live today. They lead lives where hard work and discipline take a backseat to getting things done quickly, and that's just not right.

As we aspire higher we often want our challenges to be

solved *now* rather than having the discipline to handle them in a patient and positive manner. We currently live in the micro-wave age. Just as we want microwavable food that's done in an instant, we want microwavable promotions and raises. We want microwavable profits, microwavable success. We want to be-come CEO, but without working our way up through the com-pany: microwave. (Maybe before becoming *chief* executive, you have to be an *Indian executive* first!). We want to perform at Carnegie Hall without practicing and performing at smaller ven-ues in smaller cities first: microwave. We want to get a degree in four days online rather than attending class for four years: micro-wave. As a society, we may crave the microwavable, but *real* suc-cess requires an old-school approach. The most satisfying meals often take time to produce. When my wife makes gumbo, it takes three days to prepare—and the wait is worth every minute. Trust me. If you take the time to go through the effort to live a deter-mined and disciplined life, you'll see the same type of benefits and you'll understand that true success is worth the wait. Be-cause shortcuts may require less effort, they offer only short-term successes—what I like to call *perceived* success. A friend of ours is a plastic surgeon. She sees thirty to forty people a day who want some form of cosmetic surgery: a tummy tuck, liposuction, you name it. The first thing that she encourages her clients to do is to go home. She says, "Come back and see me in six months. I want you to go and work out, change your diet." Most of them refuse. By this point in the chapter I'm sure you know why: they don't have the discipline. It takes discipline to change your diet. It takes discipline to get up an hour or two earlier in order to work out. That's the harder approach. Instead, they say, "I want you to make me twenty pounds lighter now through surgery."

Often we neglect to put the safeguards in place that might have prevented us from losing discipline in the first place. At Southern University our boys' and girls' teams traveled together. We rode the same buses and stayed in the same hotels. That could create problems, obviously. The coaches put safeguards in place to prevent the problems before they occurred. The girls rode in the front of the bus while the boys rode in the back and the coaches rode in between. At the hotels, the boys stayed at one end of the facility while the girls stayed at the other end. The coaches' rooms were in between. Safeguards. Coach Ben Jobe was not having any cohabitation on the road on his watch.

If we don't have safeguards as married men and women we will almost undoubtedly encounter problems, major problems. What those safeguards are for each of you, I can't say, but you know you. Maybe you simply can't go out for drinks with an attractive coworker because, well, you know you. Or maybe you can't spend late nights in chat rooms talking with someone of the opposite sex—even anonymously—because, well, you know you. Safeguards. They are vital for our well-being in every aspect of our lives. They keep us disciplined.

Now don't get me wrong—I believe in balance. Determination has its place, and discipline has its place. But they must exist in balance. I work, I play, I spend time with my family, I travel, I work out, but it's balanced. This is what I call my "P model": I pray in the morning; I punch the clock as a coach; I participate in family activities, and then I play.

Finally, I pass out at night. Sleep is good. All of those people who say they never sleep, well, shame on them. Consistent lack of sleep is not good. Your body needs the rest. Lack of sleep will catch up with you. It really does. It will affect your discipline, particularly your ability to think and make decisions. You have to take care of yourself mentally and physically if you want to be disciplined.

I was blessed to have discipline instilled in me early by my parents, Inez and Jim Johnson. It got me through high school and college, through some of the most difficult times in my life. I was really lucky to have two loving parents, and I know a lot of people aren't as lucky. Not having a father around unfairly *misplaces* the burden on the mother, because she has to play both roles to the children. Then the kids feel *displaced*, because they do not receive the benefits of having both parents in the home, and that can lead to a lack of discipline. That lack of discipline can prevent our children from aspiring higher and achieving their dreams. Heck, sometimes it prevents them from even having dreams, and that's truly sad.

Now, I know that there are plenty of single mothers raising sons and daughters the right way, who are instilling the discipline and values that will allow them to become successful adults. But their challenge is great, and for many it is simply too difficult to overcome. Therefore, to all you absent men: Get back in the home. Become the safeguard your family needs. The lack of discipline, and the displacement caused by your absence, affects you and your family. And whatever affects your family, affects your community. And whatever affects your community, affects our world.

I never had a problem staying disciplined. Part of that was because of my parents, but another part was maybe because I always thought I wasn't good enough. I don't mean that in a negative way; I mean it in an inspiring way. I never had a negative mindset that was self-limiting and would have prevented me from aspiring higher. I just mean that I always felt like I had something to prove, which really motivated me. As a result, I was disciplined enough to not allow the challenges and distractions that come along in life to sway me from my quest.

As a player, if I wasn't the first one in the gym in the morning, I was angry that somebody else beat me. Even today, when I'm not the first coach in the office, I'm disappointed. I always want to feel I'm outworking everybody. There are times during the season when I even sleep in the office, but working long hours should not be a lifestyle. It might be necessary once in a while to be the person who turns out the lights for a few nights in order to finish an important project or meet a critical deadline. But some people, regardless of circumstance, just *have* to be the first person in the office in the morning and the last to leave at night, every night. Listen up: Working twenty hours a day every day is not the way to aspire higher. Rather, that's going to throw off the balance I talked about, and lead to a burnout. Let's be honest: Some people do that because they don't want to go home; they might have a deeper problem. As for me, I like sleeping next to my wife.

In my business, teaching players to have discipline on the court can be difficult because, just as in life, sometimes the disciplined play may contradict human instinct. On defense we tell players to stay down and don't jump when an opponent pump fakes, because if they get caught in the air, it can set off a chain of events that are all bad for the team. It opens up opportunities for the shooter to dribble past you and penetrate the defense. The player may then attract other defenders, which creates opportunities for him to pass to a wide-open teammate. All bad. Or it may open up an opportunity for offensive rebounds, because you and your teammates are out of position. All bad. That's the kind of havoc that failing to display discipline—in this case, the simple act of going for a pump fake—can create. You and your teammates are displaced, and so you get "dissed." You get dissed because you're out of position. Being out of position means that you're off the course needed to reach your goal.

Only discipline will keep you on that course. You've got to remember that life is not just about *you*. That's why you've got to be disciplined enough to stay in position. It's why you have to stay down on pump fakes. When you get out of position it makes you ineffective, affects everything you do and everything you want, and derails your ability to aspire higher.

One of the most disciplined defensive players I've ever seen was Michael Cooper, the great Los Angeles Laker who was the nemesis of some of the greatest players in the 1980s, including Larry Bird. Coop wasn't a great ball handler, but he could knock down open threes—critical threes. But more importantly, he was great on defense. He gave some of the best players of his generation fits on the court because he always knew where to be. His job was usually to guard the other team's best player, much like Mario Elie, my former teammate on the 1999 Spurs championship team. When our coaches would design a trapping defense against an opponent's top scorer, Mario would say, "I got him by myself," and he almost always did. But the rare times he didn't, we had a safeguard; we called him 5-0: David Robinson. Mario and I would guard guys real tight. When we were right up on them, Mario would start talking: "You can drive if you want," he said. "Five-oh is gonna block that shit." Five-oh was our last safeguard. Michael Cooper always knew his position, Mario Elie always knew his position, and David Robinson definitely always knew his position.

When you're in the right position, those who do not want you to succeed suddenly become concerned. Once that defensive player leaves the floor, the offense no longer worries about him. He's no longer a threat to the play. But when you remain in position you remain effective. When your company is in the right position, your competitors are concerned. When your attitude is in the right position, those who thought you'd allow challenges and frustrations to distract you from your goals are suddenly worried.

When I arrived in the NBA with Seattle in 1988, I was one of the most disrespected players in the league. Sure, I was on the team but in the minds of most guys in the league, I was not a threat. What harm could I do when I was not even on the court most of the time? When I became head coach of the Mavericks in 2005, we were not respected as true title contenders. Sure, we scored a lot of points, but people weren't really concerned about us. They were concerned about the Spurs; they were concerned about Detroit; they were concerned about Miami. Not us.

Our competitors did not respect us because although we had a lot of victories, they were victories without physicality, without the type of defense it takes to win championships. Winning in our league is done through defense, and defense is physical. It's true that that was a chink in our armor when I started as coach. We were not a determined defensive team, and we did not yet have the disciplined mind-set necessary to be one. Not yet. My first order of business was to change that. If you want to change your life, you first must be determined in your goals and develop the discipline to reach them.

This will help you in the pursuit of your goals; it will help your company; it will strengthen your faith. A lack of discipline will be detrimental to your finances, to your friendships, to your fitness, to your life. Let's look at some examples: People who file for bankruptcy say, "I over-mortgaged myself. I over-financed myself." Not enough discipline. You look at children who haven't been successful in sports. They might say, "I didn't work hard enough. I was supposed to take more shots, swim more laps, get in better condition." Not enough discipline. A golfer who loses a tournament by a stroke or on the final hole in match play might say, "I should have hit more balls or spent more time on the putting green." Not enough discipline.

Discipline will make a big difference in your results. Too many people try to rely on talent alone. In basketball, let's say there's a guy who averages eighteen points a game on an average team, but he never really works that hard; he just comes to practice and goes home. If he spent a little more time in the weight room, studied a little more game film, stayed a little longer after practice, maybe he'd be averaging twenty-two points a game on a great team. It's all about having the discipline to put in a little more time—*quality* time, not quantity time—on your skills. It's the same for the salesman, the teacher, or the entrepreneur. Disciplined, quality time will always reap higher rewards.

Sometimes you need a little help to have the discipline to succeed. For me, one guy who really helped me was Kenny Smith, my former Houston teammate who is currently a broadcaster on TNT. He was one of the hardest-working players I ever witnessed. We shot 1,000 to 1,500 shots a night when nobody was around, because back then my jump shot was poor. He used to tell me my jump shot was sick and needed to be healed. He said, "Boy, if you can just develop a little sixteen-foot J you could have a good NBA career." We tipped the security guard at our home arena, The Summit, because he needed to turn the lights on for us. K.S. worked me like he was mad at me. I shot so many jumpers I didn't want to shoot another one in my life, but it made me a better player. Forget that: It kept me in the league and allowed me to earn millions and experience winning a championship. Thanks, K.S.

To him, discipline was about having a plan. He once said to me,

> Every day I had to shoot a certain amount of jumpers. It became a routine. Every day in high school I had to study a certain amount of time, and the more I studied, the more I could play basketball. As a kid, I had a routine as well. If I studied for three hours, I could play basketball

for an hour. If I studied for six hours, I could play basketball for two hours. It was all about routine. Setting a routine and then getting rewarded. I felt I wasn't going to get rewarded if I didn't have the routine.

The result? "When I came out to shoot a jump shot, I felt the shot was going in because of my routine." If you have a routine, you have discipline.

Discipline stretches you. For years my son. Avery Jr., only dribbled with his right hand, which I was trying to change. He said, "Daddy, why do I have to dribble with my left hand?" Now he dribbles with his left and understands why: because a good defender will always take away the right hand. Now he says, "Daddy, you were right about developing that left hand." Golfers should understand how important it is to add discipline to their games, to add shots to their repertoires. You might wonder why you need to learn how to slice. There'll be times you're going to have to hit around a tree. Why do I need to learn how to hit a hook? Same reason. (Hey, with my golf game, I'm behind trees a lot.)

I've heard stories about Tiger Woods and how he practices an hour and a half or two hours with just a nine iron. Discipline. He learned discipline from his late father, Earl, an Army officer, and he has always disciplined himself—because he had a higher vision for which he wanted to be prepared: "When I'm at Augusta, when I'm at the U.S. Open, when I'm at the British Open, I'm going to need this nine iron to hit a specific shot with a specific spin, and I'm going to have to hit it under pressure." Believe me, when that theoretical situation becomes a reality, you're going to be a lot better off if you've imagined it several hundred times in practice.

Discipline also helps your decision making. As a player, I prided myself on having one of the best assist-to-turnover ratios in the game. I had to make sound decisions with the basketball. I would study hours of film of the guy guarding me until I knew all of his strengths and weaknesses, and his tendencies. I knew whether he would guard me close or play the passing lanes. I knew whether he went to his left or his right. I knew how disciplined *he* was in going for pump fakes. It wasn't easy. I had to spend hours watching film of every other starting point in the league *and* his backup; not the most exciting thing to do when you're an NBA player. But that young kid who felt he always had something to prove? He never disappeared.

THREE

Decisions

YOU'VE BEEN DETERMINED IN THE PURSUIT of your goal. You're disciplined and not easily distracted by things that could diminish your chances of success. Now it's decision time. The decisions you make as you aspire higher will have a profound effect on your destiny. They might affect you today or maybe not for several days—or longer. But hear me now: The decisions you make today will impact tomorrow, just as the decisions you made yesterday and the day before affected your life today. Tomorrow is a direct result of today.

Hear this, too: There are no small decisions. In fact, the best decision you can make today—any day—is to elevate the importance of the details—the small, fine details of your life. Pay attention to the small stuff. Forget those who tell you not to sweat the small stuff. Sweat it.

What kind of details? They're all around you. Start by asking yourself: What time am I getting to work every day? Am I getting there before my boss? What time am I leaving at the end of the day? Is there something else I can do before I leave that will put me—and more importantly, the business—ahead of my competition tomorrow? Who am I socializing with? Are they supportive of my aspirations, or are they people who are jealous, people who want to see me stumble, fall, and fail? How late do I stay up each night? Am I getting the proper amount of sleep? Am I working out? What am I watching on television? What am I listening to on the radio? Am I taking a vacation? Am I at least creating some "me" time in order to refuel and refocus? What do I drink? Is my resume up to date? Are my computer skills in tune with the new technology?

Are you starting to get the idea? The answers to these questions will offer you a picture of the details of your life. They might seem small, but how you respond to each question, and—more importantly—how you change your actions will either boost or diminish the gains to be made through determination and discipline.

Details. Details. Details. Decisions.

You make more decisions in a day than you know. You make most of them without thinking. You've just been making those kinds of decisions so long they don't feel like decisions. It's an instinct; it's a habit. But think about this: If nothing changes, nothing changes. If you're not where you want to be, consider how you got there, and whether the first decision you have to make is to start making different decisions, beginning today. One decision I made a few years ago was to stop overreacting emotionally when things didn't happen the way I wanted them to happen. When my children were young, it would freak me out when one of them got a bad grade on a test. I reacted like the whole world had come to an end. I decided that I had to stop doing that, because my reaction wasn't making things any better. I was not getting the desired result. So instead, I tried to offer constructive criticism. I told them maybe they needed to change their study habits or their listening habits in class. When nothing changes, nothing changes. Most importantly, I had to stop acting like they had failed the bar exam. It was not accomplishing anything.

There are also bigger decisions, the ones requiring thought and contemplation. The ones you know are critical to your aspirations. Should I leave my job? Should I propose to her? Should I accept his proposal? Should I go back to school? Should I start going to church? Should I follow my heart and teach when I could make more money doing something else?

Most of your decisions are driven by common sense and an innate sense of right and wrong. No matter where you are spiritually, you know the difference. We all know the difference. We know the difference between what we want to do and what we should do. I hate going to the mall with my wife. I'm too impatient. She and my daughter can spend two hours in one store and not buy anything, or spend fifteen minutes in another store and buy too much. But every now and then I have to go, even though I hate it. It's not what I *want* to do, but it's what I should do because it makes my wife feel good, and besides, when I get home there might be a little surprise for me.

As a player, I didn't like training camp, but of course I had to go, and I had to go with a good attitude. When we started flying on private planes I got spoiled and I didn't like it when we had to fly commercial. I didn't like getting my ankles taped, but it was a precaution, something necessary to prevent a serious injury. Very often you have to make the decision to just go ahead and do something that you don't want to do because you know it's the right thing to do. Sure, many decisions are not black and white. Often it's difficult to discern what is right, to know whether your decision will move you along your path of higher aspirations. On those occasions, we often make our decisions based on faith—on, as the Bible puts it, a thing "hoped for" and yet "not seen."

Each of our decisions is based on our experiences—what we've seen and what we've learned throughout our lives. Those experiences have made us all smarter than we may believe. And yet we still sometimes make bad decisions, very bad decisions. I've made bad decisions. Why? Why do we make destructive decisions that we know will prevent us from reaching our goal—or at least delay it? First and foremost, we're human, and we all fall short of where God wants us to be.

I also think bad decisions are caused by one's state of mind. A mind clouded by negativity will not produce sound decisions. Some negativity comes from within us. For any number of reasons, we just may not believe in ourselves enough to make the right decision. Insecurity can often lead to bad decisions. But most often, our negativity is caused by external forces: negative events and especially negative people.

Winners surround themselves with other winners and people who want to see them win: their spouses, their friends, their coworkers. For a successful person, all those people are going to be winners, or people who want to be on a winning team. Winners are never surrounded by losers—people who are either out to steal the success of others, who have stopped aspiring higher themselves, or who simply don't want to see someone else win. We all know them. They're people who stagnate. They're the first to cry, "Poor me." They're the ones who prejudge people by the color of their skin—Black or White or something in between. Yet they are the ones who are probably lacking in determination and discipline, and they certainly aren't making smart decisions. Listen: All White people aren't bad, and neither are all African Americans or Hispanics. All athletes are not dumb. Anyone who thinks otherwise possesses a loser's mentality. For anything in their lives that isn't going the way they'd like it to, the fault lies with everybody but them.

And then there are the folks who simply have no will to compete—let alone win—on their own, and don't want to see you win, either. I call those folks "treadmill people." They're just running in place. They never get off the treadmill. Like runners who never go outside to test themselves against the elements and obstacles that lie on a street, or a running trail, or even a track. They're always on their own treadmill, running in place and going nowhere. Those are the people who try to affect your decisions with their poisonous attitude. They consist of the coworker who says: "I've been doing this job for 30 years; they'll never promote you." They're the middle-level manager who envies your gifts and focuses on your weaknesses instead of your strengths. They're the coach who doesn't play you because you don't fit his idea of an athlete. For many years, that's what happened to African-American quarterbacks. They didn't fit the profile of what coaches thought a "real" quarterback was—they didn't think an African-American quarterback could be a leader. Too many coaches had a truncated view of what a quarterback was supposed to look like and that view did not include African Americans. But Doug Williams changed all that in 1988, with his historic performance in Super Bowl XXII. Today my son and his generation are growing up when the position finally has no color. Even the sidelines have no color these days, as evidenced by the historic appearance of two Black head coaches—Tony Dungy of the Indianapolis Colts and Lovie Smith of the Chicago Bears—in Super Bowl XLI. Today, African-American kids can aspire to be Time Warner Chairman (and former CEO) Richard Parsons, or Kenneth Chenault, CEO of American Express, because the Fortune 500 corner office no longer has any color, either. Caucasian kids can aspire to be Steve Nash, John Stockton, or Dirk Nowitzki because those players have shown that the NBA is not restricted to only Black players. And kids from all over the world can aspire to play in the NBA because of guys like Manu Ginobili, Tim Duncan, Leandro Barbosa, and Andrea Bargnani. The world is a much better place when what we aspire to be isn't defined by color, only by our gifts and our desire to succeed.

You are in control of what you want to be—but not if you're surrounded by treadmill people. People like the spouse, or lover, or boss who belittles you because of their own insecurities. They will disturb and distort, or even try to derail your efforts to achieve your dream.

I hated playing with treadmill guys. Generally, they were the ones who'd just gotten a big contract. That's when they jumped on the treadmill. You could see it in the way they talked to team-mates. You could see it in their work habits. They didn't have the same fire, the same punch, or the same drive. The summer be-fore the last year of their contract, they would be in tip-top shape, with almost no body fat. The summer after they got the big deal, they'd show up overweight and lazy, and they'd be surrounded by individuals who share the treadmill way of thinking: people reminding them that they're getting paid and maybe now they don't have to work so hard. I hated it. Golden State gave me my first fully guaranteed contract for the 1993–94 season, my sixth year in the league; it was worth $300,000. I thought that was something back then. Seven years later, the Spurs signed me to a one-year deal worth $8 million. I was nearing the end of my play-ing career, and it was kind of a reward for years of hard work—and the championship, of course. Did I become the treadmill guy anywhere along the way as my salary soared? Please. It was never in me. Being the treadmill guy was never in my DNA. If you feel like you have the potential to become a treadmill person, you're going to have to be very careful to surround yourself with the right kind of people, the kind who aspire higher. You'll have to eliminate certain negative people from your life, or their go-nowhere "treadmill" mentality will infect your decisions. You need to distance yourself from those people.

How do you do that? Begin by asking yourself these questions: With this person in my life, am I winning or losing? What sorts of things are they saying to me? The answer to the second question will help you answer the first one. What the people closest to you are saying to you every day has a profound effect on your state of mind and, in effect, your success. What flows into your ears gets in your mind and has an effect on how you behave. So the question is: Are the words these people are saying to me making me a winner or a loser? As I said, the answer to this question will make the first one a no-brainer. If that person is filling your ears with negativity, they've got to go. If you want to win, you've got to eliminate losers from your life.

When I was in college, there was a lot of drinking in my life. I engaged in out-of-control drinking, and a lot of my so-called friends did, too. During my rookie year in the NBA, I had to eliminate people who wanted to continue to drink out of control. There will be friends and even family members who may influence you to be out of control in some aspect of your life. You'll have to eliminate these individuals, or at least keep yourself from them until you can get under control. Continuing to associate with them simply because they're friends or family will only perpetuate your bad habit. Just because you eliminate them doesn't mean you have to stop loving them, caring for them, praying for them, or being there for them when they need you. But in order to get under control, you must move them out of your life—at least for a while.

During my first stint with San Antonio, there was one guy on the team who was always saying something bad about the coach, Larry Brown. His game plan was bad. His rotation was bad. His practices were bad. Every day, it was something. The coach could not do anything to satisfy him. I could not allow that kind of thinking to potentially affect my behavior. Since I couldn't trade or cut him, I did the only thing I could do as a player: I moved my locker. I "eliminated" him the best way I could.

When it comes to our children, sometimes we have to make decisions for them that will keep them away from a negative influence. A couple of years ago, Avery Jr. had a friend who always spoke disrespectfully to his father. Instead of calling him Dad or something similar, he called him by his first name. One day, Avery Jr. asked me if he could have a play date with the kid. I said no. I did not want that boy's spirit of disobedience and lack of respect to influence *my* son.

Making the decision to eliminate people from your life can be painful. They may be lifelong friends. Their belief systems, their morals, or the way they see life might change—for reasons that likely have little or nothing to do with you. They might hurt you. They might steal from you. They might begin to put their own interests ahead of yours. Eliminating them from your life will no doubt be difficult, but it might be necessary. That doesn't mean you can't embrace them again at some point in the future, but for now, elimination must mean elimination. I'm not talking about hostility, just elimination.

I feel the same about family. As I mentioned in Chapter 1, Determination, just because they are related to you by blood doesn't mean they have the same spirit. I care about people, and I want to help others go higher, but if they don't have my spirit, I cannot always be there for them. They may have my name, but that's not the same as my spirit. I don't think everybody in your family has the same spirit as you. As painful as it may be, you may need to eliminate some of them, too.

Changes—even painful ones—are going to be necessary at various points along your journey. If you keep making the same decisions that have prevented you from aspiring higher, you're going to get the same results. As I've said, if nothing changes, nothing changes.

I'm fortunate to be a blessing in the lives of many people, but if I find out someone is a liability, if they're draining me financially, spiritually, or emotionally, they've got to go. I don't make the decision lightly and I always try to do it when I am in my best frame of mind. When you're trying to decide who's in your inner circle, you want to be at your spiritual and emotional best. I try to make my critical decisions about people when I'm in what I call my "overflow stage." What does that mean? Think of your emotional tank like a gas tank, measured by a meter. After you go to the gas station for a fill-up, the meter will typically move just past "full." That's what I call the "overflow."

When my emotional meter is past full I'm in a good place. I

don't want to make a critical decision when I've had a bad day at the office, a disagreement with my wife, or after we've played a bad game. I don't want to do it when I'm at my lowest moment emotionally. This is when my tank is running on fumes, and I feel emotionally drained. I don't like to talk to my team right after a game because it's such an emotional time. I speak to them the next day instead. I have to talk to the media right after the game, but I try to speak to them only in short sentences because I'm so emotional. I don't want to say the wrong thing. I want to make the best decisions I can, and that means I make them in the overflow stage.

If you want to make decisions in the right state of mind, you certainly can't make them when you're drunk. How many babies are born because decisions were made when two people were high or intoxicated? How many decisions are made when people are in a bad mood, or when a loved one has died? They weren't past full. They were filled with anxiety and grief. We've all been there. Haven't you ever told yourself after making a bad decision, "Man, if I had it to do all over again. . . ." State of mind. What you're really saying is, if you were in the right state of mind, you would not have made that same decision.

When it comes to decisions, just because you make a good one doesn't always mean you're going to get the result you were looking for, and that's okay. If you keep making good decisions, good results are going to follow more often than not; just not every time. For example, much has been made of the decision I made last spring to start a "small" lineup against the Golden State Warriors in the first round of the playoffs. Typically, we start Erick Dampier at center. He's 6' 11", a traditional low-post center. But the Warriors don't play anything traditionally. Nellie—Warrior coach Don Nelson—never did anything traditionally; his style is even called Nellie Ball. First and foremost he takes the center out of the game. He plays four small guys and a big guy who's not a traditional center, but more of a power forward who can run the floor. Offensively he uses those almost-interchangeable parts to spread the floor and take a quick shot before the defense can get set. His teams shoot lots of threes, run isolations, and post-ups. It's simple stuff, but if run correctly, over and over, it can be effective. The game becomes their "will" against your "won't." Defensively, he uses a lot of gimmicks. He'll use some zone, some traps. His teams make you shoot quickly because they want to run.

I loved it when I was playing Nellie Ball as a member of the Warriors during the 1993–94 season. The starting lineup was me, Latrell Sprewell, Chris Mullin, Billy Owens, and at center, Chris Webber, who would play power forward most of his career. It may have been the best team Nellie ever had. Webber was Rookie of the Year. Sprewell was first-team all-NBA. Nellie Ball helped me to really get to the point where I understood what I needed to do offensively. It taught me how to operate and how to be an aggressive scorer. It gave everybody a chance to score and was fun to play.

I always loved playing with a true center, and I always coach with a true center, but I did not want to fall victim to Nellie Ball, and I believed we could outplay them at their own game. So for game one I replaced Dampier in the starting lineup with 6'7"

Devean George, and slipped Dirk Nowitzki to center. The lineup was nothing new to us. We practiced it throughout the season and used it in small stretches during games. In fact, after losing our first four games of the season, we got our first win against Phoenix using that small lineup. Was it a good decision to use that lineup in game one against the Warriors? Strategically, yes; philosophically it was right, but mentally, who knows? We lost game one 97–85 at home, but the loss had nothing to do with whom we started; we lost because we shot 35 percent from the floor, well below our average, and we missed a ton of layups. We missed fourteen of twenty-one layups—point-blank layups! That had nothing to do with the starting lineup. We won game two, but went to Oakland and lost two games in front of the loudest crowds there since I was a Warrior in 1993–94. As a matter of fact, the reason they were so loud was because the team had not made the play-offs since that 1993–94 season. Down three games to one, we just couldn't get to game seven back at home. One of my coaches, Popeye Jones, may have said it best when he said the Warriors played as if they'd been eating soup with a fork. They were hungry.

If I had it to do over, would I start the same lineup? Yes. But hopefully this season we'll be able to play big, medium, or small— and be comfortable either way.

Making good decisions is not a skill we're born with. We all need to learn how to do it. A few years ago my wife and I attended a parent–teacher night at a new school our children were attending outside Houston. One of the teachers told the parents: "We want to help your child with critical thinking. We're not concerned about their grades. We're concerned about their critical thinking."

I was blown away—in a good way. Why? Because education, no matter the grade level, should be about critical thinking. Without critical thinking, you can't make good decisions. Once students get out of college, their success is not determined by the grades they received in elementary, middle school, high school, or even college. It's determined by their ability to be critical thinkers. So if you do not pursue the process of positive, critical thinking early, the more difficult it will be to embrace it later in life when it matters most.

Having majored in psychology affects the way I coach. It helped me understand the brain and the behavior of the individual. Most of the time I'm not just coaching basketball. At times I have to deal with anxiety, depression, or relationship issues. Coaches constantly have to deal with the mental and emotional development of young people. Majoring in psychology gave me that foundation to have a better understanding of those emotions. I call upon those lessons every day.

Players want to make more money, so they get anxious when they're not playing well or when they're on the bench. There's a huge spirit of disappointment that must be managed. Some players are really insecure. They think I don't respect them, or don't care about them. Any manager or coach is always dealing with those issues. If you're a manager, you already know that there's a certain way you must talk to every individual in your office, and you often have to spend time with each staff member. When it comes to a non-basketball issue, I treat each individual differently. I may give one guy a book, another guy a music CD, another guy a sermon—something related to whatever he's dealing with. I may take another player to dinner or lunch. I might give a guy a restaurant gift certificate for him and his wife. I have to have a different way to touch each individual, and not just in my workplace, but also in my family life. Some of my family members need a phone call, while others might need a loan. Their needs vary and it's my job to sort out who needs what. Psychology. It's life.

Are all people who do bad things bad people? Look at the list of athletes with notorious pasts, from Mike Tyson to Michael Vick. Are they bad people, or did they make bad decisions? They made bad decisions because they didn't distance themselves from losers. Tyson didn't distance himself from the life he lived prior to being discovered by the late trainer Cus D'Amato and molded into the heavyweight champion of the world. Vick ultimately made the decision to continue participating in something that cost him his job—and more than $70 million in earnings. He should have decided to separate himself from the dog-fighting culture and the people who support it. Instead, he not only participated in it, but funded the operation that brought him down. I don't think they're bad people. They made bad decisions.

Of course, it isn't just athletes who make poor, life-changing, and in some cases criminal, decisions that derail their aspirations. In newspapers across the country, the business sections have been filled with the names of corporate executives whose decisions cost them millions and, in some cases, their freedom, too. Most of them were highly educated, but they made decisions based on greed rather than need. They were millionaires trying to become billionaires. They were billionaires trying to become zillionaires. When is enough, enough? They made their decisions based on money, not character.

When someone has that kind of unquenchable need for money, it's usually just greed. But when you have a satisfied spirit—one that is satisfied with the people around you, with your own accomplishments, and with your higher aspirations—there's no need to be greedy.

Through my faith, I know what the Bible says: "What God has for me, He has for me, and no one else." On the flip side, "What others possess is not meant for me, so I should not be jealous of someone else's possessions or achievements." I'm at peace with that truth, but if there's room to go higher, if there's a chance He has even more for me, then I'm going there. But I'm going with integrity of spirit, and with the people around me who are supportive of my aspirations. I'll do my best and He'll do the rest.

I'm trying to aspire higher, but if I don't achieve the goals and aspirations I've created for myself I'll still be satisfied—because I know I'm doing my best. For three straight summers starting when I was ten years old, my dad entered me in the NFL's "Punt, Pass, and Kick" competition in our area. The first year I went, I must have come in 100th place; the second year, maybe 50th place. My dad was disappointed. "Son, I've seen you throw the ball in front of our house and in the park," he said. "I've seen you throw it and kick it, so I know you're not doing your best." I thought he was mad at me for not winning, but he was just upset because I didn't do my best. When I was thirteen, I came in third. "Son," he told me. "I'm proud of you." "But dad," I said. "I didn't win." He replied, "But you did your best." That story is one of my great memories of my dad. That was the best I could do and it was good enough for him.

The higher you aspire, the more difficult your decisions become. Everybody wants to be the head coach of the Mavericks but they don't want to make my most difficult decisions. Who do I cut? Who plays? Who takes the last-second shot? What play do we run?

Everyone wants to be Berkshire Hathaway CEO Warren Buffett or Microsoft cofounder Bill Gates, but you don't want their challenges and difficulties. They have decisions to make every day that can affect billions of dollars, as well as the financial well-being of thousands of people, employees, and stockholders.

People envy Mark Cuban's money, but they don't want his difficulties. Trust me, despite his millions—I mean billions, $2.6 billion, says *Forbes*—you don't really want to be MC. First of all, you probably couldn't take the heat he takes every day for speaking out against some of the things he believes are wrong with the NBA. He's been fined a lot by the NBA for what they consider inappropriate behavior. They—and I stress *they*—don't believe he wants to be part of the "team." The perception is that he's trying to reinvent the wheel. Well, that's good. Nothing is perfect. Any "wheel" can stand a bit of "reinventing" every so often. Additionally, MC has to make decisions every day that can affect the value of the Mavericks. A bad decision can kill the value of the brand and the franchise. Despite what most people might think based on what they see in public, MC is not a big-time emotional guy. He doesn't make snap decisions affected by emotions. When he decided to hire a young guy with no experience as a head coach—me—that decision was well thought out and not made lightly. When he selects certain individuals to run his business—guys like Mavericks president Terdema Ussery, an African American who may not have been given that opportunity by some other franchise—it's a well-thought-out decision. His decisions—and actions—may be unconventional. They could succeed in a big way, but they could also fail in a big way. Most people don't want that much on their shoulders.

Whether it's an entrepreneur like MC; a Fortune 500 CEO like Gregg L. Engles of Dean Foods, a global dairy product and food company that does $2.6 billion in revenue and employs 2,700 people worldwide; or a real estate developer like Donald Trump; there are major difficulties that go with the decisions they have to make every day.

Before you can decide just how high you want to aspire, make the decision to study yourself. Get to know yourself. I did that early in my NBA career. I was questioned by the owners and coaches I played for, and I spent an enormous amount of time with people who were successful outside of sports. They'd ask me: Who are you? Where are you going? What is your purpose? What is your passion? What do you want to do that won't feel like work? They cared about me, so I began to study myself and answer those questions. I decided that I wanted to be a coach. I also wanted to make a lot of money so I could have an impact on as many people as is humanly possible. Knowing yourself provides clarity. It helps you make better decisions.

Too many people take too long trying to "find themselves." They change majors twelve times, hop from job to job, or continue to try quick-fix business schemes that get them nowhere. There are even church hoppers—those who hop from one church to another, but never commit to a church family. They hop and get nowhere.

As you aspire higher, it's critical that you get to know your strengths and weaknesses, desires, vulnerabilities, insecurities, and your plusses and minuses. This way, you'll know what you have to work on. Then you can look to others to help you improve yourself. That process of looking to others for help—and in turn helping others on their journeys—is critical to aspiring higher.

Sound decisions are contagious because what you do and how you do it affects others. In Chapter 2, we talked about discipline. The words "discipline" and "disciple" come from the same roots. Disciplined leaders develop other disciplined leaders. As a great leader, you want to help create disciples of your own by being a mentor. To me, that's the greatest thing about leadership: developing other leaders. Some of my most gratifying experiences in recent years have been seeing our young point guard, Devin Harris, grow into becoming a leader on the court; having one of my assistant coaches, Sam Vincent, get his first head coaching job with Charlotte; hearing that Avery Jr. became captain of his basketball team; and seeing a pastor friend of mine, Rev. Terrence Johnson, get his own church, Higher Dimensions, in Houston. I made the decision to be there for all of them and I like to think that in some way I helped them achieve those goals by being a mentor. Being a mentor means imparting your wisdom, your influence, your knowledge, and your experiences to someone else. The idea is to have a positive effect on their lives, their family, their careers, their community, and their faith.

You won't go higher until you've made the decision to inspire other people to ascend themselves. Sure, you may find some measure of success. You may go from making $10,000 a year to $20,000; $20,000 to $100,000; $100,000 to $200,000 to $500,000, but all that money is worthless unless you help other people along the way. If you make it to a higher level, but the people around you stay on the ground, that's not good enough. This is why I have a problem with mega ministries, when the minister's financial reward does not trickle down to the congregation. If the pastor is flying in a private jet, wearing alligator shoes, and living in a $2 million house, why aren't the members reaping some benefits? If the CEO is doing well, shouldn't all the employees share the wealth? If others are not going higher with you, then to me you're making a decision to be selfish— and that's the wrong decision!

If you want to attain greatness, one of the easiest ways to do so is to have the mindset that says: *I want somebody to get on the elevator with me.* Why own an island worth hundreds of millions of dollars? Why have a Falcon 2000, or Gulf Stream 550, or Hawker 400XP or King Air jet if you're the only one on it? Enjoy it with somebody. Celebrate with somebody.

In 1985, when I was a redshirt junior at Southern, I worked for a man named Norman Chenevert. He never graduated from high school, but he owned a lumberyard in New Orleans. One day, he said he wanted to "invest in" me. When I asked why, he said, "Because you're going to be able to do something that I never can do." "What's that?"

"Graduate from college."

Mr. Chenevert told me to go to Bohn Ford and pick out an Escort. He said, "Whichever one you like, pick it out, I'm going to buy it for you." I said, "You've got to be kidding." "Pick out whichever one you like because I believe in you, I can trust you. You've been working for me in the summertime for years. You've been on time. You've never stolen anything. You've been very trustworthy." Then he said the key words, "I want to reward you. I want to help you graduate from college because if I help you graduate from college, you're going to help somebody else."

He was right. I invested in my sister's college education, my nephew's college education, and my niece's college education. My sister graduated from Dillard University in New Orleans. My niece graduated from Louisiana State University and is now a chiropractor. My nephew graduated from Southern. Had Mr. Chenevert not invested in me, maybe I wouldn't have been inspired to invest in others. It was my discipline on the job that caught his eye.

I stayed in touch with Mr. Chenevert until he died a few years ago. He was in a coma in the hospital for two weeks. I showed up at the hospital, and one hour later he died. His wife told me he needed to hear my voice one more time. We were that connected.

I was his disciple. I'm also a disciple of Bernard Griffin, my high school coach; Ben Jobe; Bernie Bickerstaff; Don Nelson; and Gregg Popovich. These men imparted wisdom to me and, in turn, I've tried to impart it to others. Mostly, though, I am a disciple of Jim Johnson, my father. His wisdom, along with the discipline and the faith in God he planted within me, has gotten me through the storms in my life.

Oh, yes, there will be storms. Even if you display unwavering determination, stay disciplined, and do your best to make good decisions, you will experience storms. You will certainly experience disappointment on the job and you may even get fired. *Storm.* You will fail to pass the bar, the securities test, or the police academy's final exam. *Storm.* You will suffer an unexpected illness. *Storm.* Somebody you thought you were a mentor to will let you down. *Storm.* You will lose a parent, a friend or, God forbid, a child. *Storm.* You will suffer a financial challenge that might cause you to lose your home. *Storm.*

Determination. Discipline. Decisions. These are the core

tenets for anyone seeking to aspire higher, but they are not immune to life; not immune to the storms.

In the next chapter, I'll share with you the storms that threatened to hinder my own aspirations, and how determination, discipline, and decisions—along with a recommitment to God that came late in my life—got me through.

FOUR

Through the Storms: My Story

GROWING UP IN NEW ORLEANS WAS a storm all by itself. I was raised in the inner city. The truth is, New Orleans is really one big inner city. I lived in the Lafitte housing projects. Drugs were everywhere. I was one of the few kids to have both a mother and a father, but they were not educated. Neither of my parents stayed in school beyond the sixth grade, though my mom got her GED when she was in her fifties. I was not exposed to much that was positive. And like every other African-American male in inner cities across the nation, I battled against statistics that were thrown in my face every day. We all knew Black males were more likely to go to jail than to college. We knew the lure of a quick fix from selling drugs was stronger than the challenge of getting an education. We knew that the stress caused by racism was likely to kill us before our time. It was tough, but at the time my parents did the best they could to keep me from knowing just how tough it was. I didn't fully know how much of a storm my life was until I became an adult.

My dad was sick a lot when I was a kid, battling heart disease. I didn't really know at the time exactly what was wrong with him; I only knew that he was often sick. There were many telephone calls to our house at odd times, when dad was at work. When my mom would hang up, we had to go to the doctor or to the hospital because he'd had another heart attack. They weren't always big ones, but each attack added to the damage. Each one made him weaker. *Storm.*

Mom and Dad were each married to other people before they met each other, so we had a blended family. There were ten children all together, and I'm number nine. I have five brothers and four sisters. My dad had six kids from his previous marriage; mom had two. We were the Black Brady Bunch, but we never considered each other stepsiblings. We were all just brothers and sisters, even though my baby sister, Andréa, and I are the only children from the union between Jim and Inez. I can't imagine raising ten kids. God bless 'em!

My mom never worked while she was married to my dad. He remodeled homes for a gentleman named Mr. Mayer. I never really knew his first name, but he was right there for my mom when my dad died and her bills escalated. Mr. Mayer really stepped up for her. He actually paid off her car loan and some of the bills my dad left behind.

Through it all, they were great parents. My dad spent a lot of time with me. He shuttled me everywhere I needed to go and made sure I knew that there was something better for me out there, as long as I got my college degree. As I wrote earlier, he knew I'd end up with a job that helped people get better. I was the second of their children to go to college, so a lot was expected of me. I know my dad's sitting in heaven, still proud of himself for recognizing early that coaching was my "gift": "I knew that kid was going to coach because he sure could talk. He was going to coach *somebody*."

My mom was funny. She didn't want to come to any of my games when I was little because she said she got too nervous. Then one day she just showed up at a game. I didn't know she was coming. The game was in progress as she came into the gym, but I saw her just before the ball was inbounded to me. I was so happy that I sprinted and got an uncontested layup—except it was in the wrong basket.

As a Black boy growing up in the 1970s in the South, having both parents was critical, and not all that common. My daddy was "Daddy" for a lot of kids in our neighborhood. After baseball or basketball practice, my dad always dropped off five or six of my teammates. When we went to McDonald's after practice, it was always with five or six other kids. When we had Sunday family dinners, there were always other kids at the table with me and my siblings. I guess when you have ten kids, another five or six does not make much of a difference. I was never jealous of my "neighborhood dad." I knew he was always *my* daddy first.

Mom and Dad used their own storms to help their children—and children from all over the projects—to learn the basic values of hard work, education, and faith. I often look back and consider them to be great teachers, and I think their lessons were well learned by a lot of kids they touched.

Back then, my biggest storm was overcoming the feeling I wrote about earlier in the book—when it seemed that I was just not good enough, not big enough, not fast enough, not smart enough. When I was thirteen, my fastball and curveball, which were the best in the city when I was nine, weren't getting anybody out any more. In basketball, I was one of the best players in what was called Biddy Ball, a league for younger kids, but during my senior year of high school I was the last man on the bench and getting no playing time—until one of my teammates got suspended right before the playoffs for breaking team rules. That allowed me to get some playing time and get noticed by some college coaches who'd come to see other guys. Tim Floyd, who later coached the Chicago Bulls, was a college coach at the time. He mentioned my name to Ron Black, the coach at New Mexico Junior College, who was coming to one of our games to see a teammate. Coach Floyd told him to look out for me, too. I was one of the few kids who had to pay to go to St. Augustine High School because I could only qualify for a partial scholarship. God got us through. That is the only way to explain it. My dad was a carpenter. He worked several jobs and somehow came up with the money. *Storms.*

I thought about going to the University of Southwestern Louisiana (now called the University of Louisiana at Lafayette), which wasn't too far from New Orleans, but I couldn't afford it, and I wasn't good enough to earn a scholarship. Not going to school was not an option. My dad had made that clear years before when he told me that he expected me to do better than he had—far better. So I had to go to school somewhere— somewhere I could play ball. *Storm.*

Coach Black liked what he saw when he came to my game. I took advantage of the opportunity I got with my teammate's suspension and proved to others what I already knew—I could play. Despite my small size and lack of pure shooting ability, I could play. I could *lead.* I could win. Coach Black saw at least some of that and offered me a full scholarship to New Mexico Junior College in a town called Hobbs. However, although I was happy to get the scholarship, I didn't want to go because I'd never been on an airplane before. I overcame my fear of flying but being at that school was a culture shock. I hated it. I didn't know this before I got there, but it was five miles from the dormitories to campus so I ended up having to hitchhike to school. The food program was terrible. There was no breakfast, lunch was just a sandwich (and even that wasn't served every day), and dinner? Please. I was never full. I got a Pell Grant but the money wasn't enough so we all pretty much had to cook for ourselves every day. Nothing much, nothing fancy. The highlight of my week was when Coach Black took me to the top local joint, Furr's Cafeteria.

The team traveled everywhere by bus. Even to games in

Arizona. I remember hurting my hip during a game in Tucson and had to make that long bus ride back in excruciating pain— 557 long miles. Coach Black was a great man, an awesome man. He did the best he could with what he had, but the living conditions were awful. One day I was late for practice, and had to hitch a ride in the back of a hearse in order to get there. As I sat back there, where there'd been Lord-knows-how-many caskets filled with dead people, I thought, "This is a message. Maybe this is not the school for me." *Storm.*

After a year at New Mexico JC—and my "dead people" experience in the back of the hearse—I transferred to Cameron University in Lawton, Oklahoma. A guy I knew from St. Augustine High School, Al, had played there and said it was a great school. He liked that it was in a military town, so there were many different types of people there. They even had dorms right on campus! I called the coach there. He obtained a video of me, offered me a scholarship, and I accepted, but it turned out to be one of the most racist situations I've ever been in. The living conditions were okay, especially compared with New Mexico JC, but I thought the teachers—especially in the accounting department where I was studying—were racist. I would go after class for tutoring but for seemingly no other reason than my race, they would not answer any of my questions. Maybe they resented me and the other Black kids being there. Most of us played sports and maybe they didn't think we deserved our spots at the school. It was just tough to be a Black kid there at that time. Period. *Storm.*

Making matters even worse, I wasn't getting any playing

THROUGH THE STORMS: MY STORY

time. The coach refused to use me. I was ten times better than our starting point guard, but who the better player was didn't matter to the coach. That man wasn't going to play me for anything—which made no sense since he brought me there. Athletically and academically, Cameron was just a bad situation for me. My passion for basketball almost died. It's a better place today—the racists are gone—but for me in 1984, along with a lot of other Black kids, it was awful. That's when I started drinking heavily. I had been drinking before, mostly with friends at parties, but now I drank a lot. In fact, I was a social alcoholic. That's when you abuse alcohol at parties and with friends, but you don't really get into trouble and, most importantly, you don't admit you have a problem. Later in life, I decided that enough was enough and I was tired of being a social alcoholic. It was, in fact, the moment when my life was saved. But then, as a lonely and frustrated Black kid in Lawton, Oklahoma, drinking was a way to forget where I was, and getting away was what I needed most. *Storm.*

In March 1985, I was watching television one night in Cameron and I saw St. John's University playing Southern University, a historically Black college based in Baton Rouge, Louisiana. It was the first round of the NCAA tournament and I fell in love with basketball again. I watched the entire game and saw the players, the coaches, the fans, and all the love they had for each other. It was another planet from where I was. I was hooked. Southern lost the game, 83–59, but I didn't care. I told myself, "That's the school where I need to be." I wanted to play Division I basketball, and after being at New Mexico JC and Cameron, I wanted to play for a Black college.

It wasn't just the appeal of going to a Black college that drew me to Southern, it was also that I was excited about going back home. Baton Rouge was just sixty-nine miles from New Orleans; my family could come see me play. And I was thrilled about the prospect of playing for a team that had just played in the NCAAs. That's what I wanted: home and big-time ball; the whole deal. I wanted to be where I didn't have to worry about whether the teachers and coaches were racists, and I wanted the opportunity to play against the top teams. I would have certainly gone to Southern right out of high school, but I wasn't good enough back then and they didn't recruit me. However, I was much better now—no thanks to New Mexico JC or Cameron. I got better in the summers when, after working all day at Crescent Plywood, I went to Xavier University, a Black college in New Orleans, to play against their players for several hours each day. Then I went to the weight room at the school and lifted. My confidence grew, too, because I was competing against good college players and more than holding my own. I was still "under construction," but I was on my way.

I'd become a better player. I had confidence in myself. Even at Cameron when nobody knew my name, I thought I could be a successful point guard. I wasn't flashy, but I knew how to get past defenders and get to the basket. No, I wasn't a great shooter, but I knew how to score. More than anything, I had *determination* on the basketball court and I knew how to make smart decisions—decisions that helped make other people look good. I knew that all I needed was a chance to play and I'd be okay. My confidence and my competence just needed an opportunity.

That proved to be one of the main storylines of my life, but it also made me who I am. It kept me hungry and humble.

My high school coach, Coach Griffin, is the reason I ended up at Southern. He suggested it might be a good place for me because both of their guards were seniors. He sent me the admissions and loan forms, then sent them in for me and I got accepted. I mostly paid my own way, even took out a $1,500 loan, and was redshirted my first season. That meant I could not play, but I could practice with the team. In the summer before school started, I showed up for the off-season pickup games with the returning players. Funny thing, though: I never got chosen to play. These guys were arrogant. They'd gotten their butts whipped by St. Johns, but they acted like they'd been to the Final Four. There was a forward on the team named Craig Pollard. He used to tell me: "We just went to the NCAAs. You won't even make the team. You're too short, you can't shoot." It was like high school all over again. *Storm.*

Once again, I used the doubts others had about me to strengthen my resolve and my determination. I knew I could play and I couldn't wait to show these guys. Until that time came, I waited. After not getting picked by the varsity guys for their pickup games, I waited until they were finished, and played against the students in their intramural games. It wasn't the best competition but I had to play any way I could. After those games I'd run around the university; that was my conditioning program. All the time, I was thinking about what I'd do when I got the opportunity to play. Finally, it came. One day Southern coach Bob Hopkins set up a game between the redshirt players and the varsity guys. It was set up like a real game, with a shot clock and referees. You probably know where this is going. I was motivated, to say the least. That high school kid who was never good enough came roaring out. That kid who got laughed at by the varsity guys went crazy. I'd had good practices before, but on this day, I was a wild man out there. I scored thirty-six points. I destroyed their whole team, including Pollard. You *know* I enjoyed that. I still smile when I think about that day. After the game, Coach Hopkins told everybody that the best point guard on campus was a redshirt: me. My name was buzzing through campus. They used to call me Ant Man, because of the way ants sneak up on you out of nowhere and then suddenly there's a swarm of them all over everything.

Though Coach Hopkins finally saw the light about me, I never got to play for him. He left Southern for Grambling the summer before I became eligible for varsity. The new coach was a guy named Ben Jobe. I'd never heard of him. He came from another Black college, Alabama A&M. One of the first things he told me was that if I couldn't shoot I couldn't play. Here we go again. *Storm.*

I told him, "I'm not a great shooter, coach, but I'm your best playmaker." He said: "Son, I don't know how that's gonna work." Clearly, I needed another argument. "Coach," I said,

If somebody shoots 50 percent from the field on jump shots, and I can shoot 60 percent from the field on layups, who gives you the most production? He makes five out of ten jumpers, and I make six out of ten layups. He's given you ten points, but I've given you twelve. Plus, I'm gonna give you some assists. I'm gonna play defense. And I'm gonna lead the team. I'm gonna do all that and sprinkle in a shot every now and then.

He said it made sense, but I'm not sure he was convinced right away. It didn't help that I got off to a slow start under his system; we had a tough early schedule. We played Kansas and St. John's. We started the season 6–9. At that point I went to Coach Jobe and told him, "I know we got off to a rough start. We've had a rough preconference schedule. If I'm going to do my best, you're going to have to loosen up on the leash. I know what I'm doing."

He listened to me, but again, Coach Jobe was not easily persuaded. "When I do something, I do it for a reason," he said. "I want my point guard to be the same way. So let me ask you about something that happened the other night. We have a player who averages thirty points, but near the end of our last game he was wide open for three straight possessions and you refused to pass to him. Why?" I said, "Coach, he missed study hall the night before and he was out partying." "Well, at least you had enough sense to let us win the game [before freezing him out.]" Coach said.

Coach liked what I had done, after he found out why. I did what I did to make a point—that the team was more important than a party, that study hall was more important than a party. I wasn't crazy; I waited until the game was well in hand before I started feeding my other teammates. He got the message. Later, so did Coach Jobe. That was a turning point in our relationship. I asked him to let me do what I do and he agreed. We won ten games in a row. Then we won the SWAC tournament, beating Grambling—and our former coach, Bob Hopkins—by fifty points in the championship game. That's still the tournament record. Imagine me—too little, can't shoot—with an NCAA Division I scoring record. I was the SWAC Player of the Year; and I was the tournament's Most Valuable Player. Very few players from historically Black colleges ever reach the NBA, even today. But despite the odds against me—in so many ways—I was thoroughly convinced that I could play in the NBA.

We lost to Temple in the first round of the 1987 NCAA Tournament in the Rosemont Arena in Chicago. Temple was coached by John Chaney. "A legend" is all I can say when it comes to Coach Chaney. I felt like I was playing against the Black Dean Smith, an icon in the game. For young African-American players growing up during that time, Georgetown coach John Thompson was our hero. He stood for Black men and for what it meant to be a strong Black man *in charge*. Both he and Chaney made all of us proud. It may be hard to imagine today, when there are so many African-American head coaches in college basketball, but just a couple of decades ago, long after the start of the civil rights movement, they were so scarce that two guys could be the icons who stood for us all.

Those were guys we looked up to. Another icon was Clarence ("Bighouse") Gaines, the beyond-legendary coach at Winston-Salem State University for forty-seven years, until he retired in 1993. He won 828 games and was at one point the highest-winning college basketball coach ever. Whenever we played them it was like going to see the pope—of Black college basketball.

John Chaney and Coach Jobe were good friends. I shook Coach Chaney's hand before that game, but that was about the nicest thing he did to me all night. He killed me with that famous match-up zone that the Owls play. It looked like there were never any driving lanes. Never. Those six layups I promised Coach Jobe? They weren't happening on that night against Temple. They beat us 75–56, and those may have been the hardest points we ever scored. The ending was disappointing, but all in all, I got everything I wanted out of that season. The whole deal. After New Mexico and Cameron, I was on top of the world as a basketball player. I was ready to prove myself yet again, at the next level, in the NBA. But, of course, there were more storms to overcome; internal storms.

At that point in my life, my spiritual faith had not yet developed—at least not on a truly personal level. When I was young I went to church, because on Sunday mornings, Daddy would say, "Let's go," and we did. When I started going to St. Augustine, a Catholic high school, I began going to Catholic church, mostly because services didn't last as long as those at the churches I'd been attending. Services at Dad's church lasted three hours. At the Catholic church, they lasted forty-five minutes. I felt good when I went to church—no matter whose it was—but I didn't want to stay for long.

Whatever my motivation, going to church more frequently got me to ask more questions about faith, and to do more soul searching. I began to really think about how much of a role faith had in my life. I wasn't Catholic and never became Catholic, but I must have made the sign of the cross a zillion times. I also probably set a record for the number of confessions for a non-Catholic. By the time I left for New Mexico JC, I had a slight sense of needing to stay connected to God. Even through the storms, I did.

At the end of my journey from New Mexico to Lawton, and finally to Baton Rouge, I went to play for the West Palm Beach Stingrays in the United States Basketball League (USBL), a professional minor league, to work on my game in preparation for the NBA draft. I was actually the first pick in the USBL draft. Okay, it was just the USBL, a minor league, but I was still the first pick. I played well and was confident I was going to get picked in the NBA draft later that summer. Still, I had a backup plan. If I didn't play well in the USBL, if I didn't play well in the predraft camps, and if I didn't get invited to an NBA training camp, I was going to go to Tulane and get my master's degree in psychology. If the NBA wasn't happening, I was going to be a sports psychologist.

Things went well enough with the Stingrays that by June I just *knew* I was going to be drafted. I told my roommate that I may not go in the first round, but the second or third round was *guaranteed*. One night I was still exhausted from having played in the Portsmouth Invitational, one of the predraft camps for potential rookies. I thought I played well there, but I was not invited to the second camp in Chicago. Nor was I invited to the Olympic trials for the 1988 team, even though the team badly needed a point guard. This was back when the Olympic team was still made up of collegiate players. Their guards were Willie Anderson of Georgia, Vernell Coles of Virginia Tech, Jeff Grayer of Iowa State, Hersey Hawkins of Bradley, Mitch Richmond of Kansas State, and Charles Smith of Georgetown—the latter was the only true point guard. The team lost to the Soviet Union in the Olympic semifinal, 82–76, before beating Australia for the bronze. I think I could have helped. After that snub, I wasn't in the best of moods as I sat in front of the television watching the draft. The first round went by as I expected. Three point guards were taken: Michigan's Gary Grant (15th), Rod Strickland from DePaul (19th), and David Rivers of Notre Dame (25th). I didn't expect to be taken ahead of any of these guys; they were all from big-time programs. I just wanted my chance.

Then the second round came and went. I was nervous, but still confident. Interestingly, Steve Kerr, a point guard from Arizona who would become my teammate eleven years later on the San Antonio Spurs championship team, was the last pick in that round, fiftieth overall.

Finally the third round began. I was still sure my name would be called, but the storm was brewing. Name after name was called. Point guards I'd never heard of were called. Point guards *you'd* never heard of were called. Twenty-five more names overall, and my name was not among them. I was not drafted. *Storm.*

I sat there in shock. My roommate said nothing. I was hurt. I was mad. I was every negative emotion imaginable. It seemed like time had stopped. However, about an hour after the draft, three teams called with offers to attend their training camps to try and make their rosters: Golden State, Portland, and Seattle. I didn't know that much about Golden State. Portland, of course, had Clyde Drexler and Terry Porter, both of whom were all-stars. I was most interested in playing for Seattle because I'd done my homework. They had just been burned in the playoffs by a small point guard, 5' 10" Michael Adams of Denver, and they were looking for a small point guard themselves. Coach Jobe said I'd have the best chance to make it in Seattle. When Seattle coach Bernie Bickerstaff called, he said he'd give me a chance. That's all I wanted—a chance.

The calls didn't totally ease the pain of not being drafted or end the shock, but getting invited to an NBA camp was at least something—it was an opportunity. In the end, whether I was a third-round draft pick or an undrafted invitee, that's all I needed and wanted: an opportunity. I played on the Sonics' summer-league team and entered every game with a single mission: I was dead set on showing everyone how wrong they were in not drafting me. I was going to destroy every other team. And I did. I penetrated defenses and dished for assists. I scored, and I played defense like a madman. Later, during my NBA career, I got tagged with the nickname Taz—as in the old Looney Tunes cartoon character, the Tasmanian Devil. If you remember him—known for his speed, ravenous appetite, and crazed behavior—then you have a pretty good idea how I played that summer. I was named co-MVP of 1988 NBA summer league.

So I survived rookie camp and played reasonably well during training camp, but I was in no position to feel confident.

There were twelve roster spots at that time, but eleven of the players had guaranteed contracts. That left only one open spot. *One.* I worried every day and played every game like I might get cut right after the final buzzer. One night, before the fourth or fifth preseason game, head coach Bernie Bickerstaff told me he was going to sit me out. I was nervous as hell. In my mind, it was another storm. This time, though, it wasn't really anything. Sometimes coaches just need to look at other players; I know that now.

During camp, all of us young players would catch a taxi to practice from the hotel, and we'd share it with a veteran. Usually I rode with John Lucas, the team's starting point guard and one of the most passionate players I have ever played with or for (he later became an NBA coach, and coached me during one of my stints with the San Antonio Spurs). One day toward the end of camp, I jumped into the cab with John, but the rest of the guys were still in the restaurant. I said, "John, we can't go, the guys aren't here." He said, "Be quiet, young fella, the axe is falling." I didn't have a clue what he was talking about. "John, we can't leave for practice," I said. "We need to wait for the other guys." "Shut up young fella," he said. "The axe is falling."

Finally, the cab took off. We got into the locker room and the other young guys weren't there. I got out onto the court, and while we were warming up I quietly counted the players. One, two, three . . . nine, ten. . . . I was still counting when Bernie called everyone together. "Now before we get started," he said, looking at me. "Let's congratulate the young fella for making the team." Everybody started clapping. What did I do? Did I keep my cool?

Of course not! I ran around the gym three times screaming my head off. Sometimes you've just got to be happy. Sometimes you've just got to let it all hang out and let the world know how you feel. That was my time.

All during that practice, I thought about all the storms I had experienced in my life and how they were suddenly all worth it. Sitting on the bench and not playing at St. Augustine was worth it. The long bus ride in excruciating pain and the lack of resources at New Mexico JC were worth it. Not playing at Cameron was worth it. Not getting picked to play during the summer before attending Southern was worth it. Not getting drafted by an NBA team was worth it. Maintaining my faith the best that I could was worth it. I still had a problem with alcohol, and I was not as good a person as I knew I should be, but I knew how to treat people. Along with my own determination, discipline, and smart decision making, I think that has long been one of the primary reasons for my success.

When it comes to people, you reap what you sow. It doesn't always look that way these days when we see people who *don't* live right still reap great financial rewards. A lot of my spiritual friends ask: Why do unkind people get blessed? Why do people who are unloving, lazy, and disrespectful get blessed? Why do people who are not passionate about the positives in life get blessed? This is my view: Those people may have material wealth, but I don't know if they are truly blessed. Who really knows that? But this I know: If our private life lines up with our public life, we will be blessed.

Team chapels helped me through my rookie season. I didn't

play often. I played in only forty-three of the eighty-two games, and when I did get to take off my sweats it wasn't for very long. Bernie had what he called the "Thirty rule": If we were up by thirty or down by thirty, I'd get to play. Sometimes when we were getting beaten in the fourth quarter and it was clear we weren't going to win, I silently rooted for us to get beaten *really* badly so I could get into the game. I know it wasn't right, but I wanted to play.

I played my first game in Sacramento against the Kings. We were winning and I scored my first points against Kings guard Vinny Del Negro, who later became my teammate in San Antonio. It was a right-handed layup, but I switched hands on him—left to right. It was a pretty move. Everybody on the team was excited for me. Later in the season, I remember being on the floor against guys I'd watched and admired when I was in college—guys like Detroit point guard Joe Dumars, who was also from New Orleans. I recall my first games against Larry Bird, Robert Parish, Kevin McHale, and the rest of the Boston Celtics; my first games against Magic Johnson and the Lakers. When the Lakers came to Seattle they had more fans than we did; it was like a home game for them. I guess it was like that for them all over the country—except maybe in Boston. I envisioned someday being on their level, but didn't really know if I'd get there. I averaged fewer than seven minutes per rare appearance.

Thank God for the chapels, which occurred before every game. Guys from both teams gathered in a room somewhere in the arena. A team chaplain or a player read some Bible verses. Guys might share some stories about their struggles. We'd pray, and that was that. They were like the Catholic services: short and sweet and you still got the spiritual message. But right after my rookie year it became clear to me that short and sweet wasn't working for me; maybe I *wasn't* getting the message. I was attending church on Sunday, but was a totally different person Monday through Saturday. And I didn't like that person. I was still a social alcoholic, and still in denial about it. The summer following my first season, in July 1989, I fell asleep while driving my car across the Mississippi River Bridge from downtown New Orleans to the "west bank" of the city. The car hit the side of the bridge—bam!—and woke me up, along with my friend, who was riding with me. He'd fallen asleep, too. When we crashed he slapped me: "What are you doing? Wake up!" he said. We could have died; I should have died. I woke up before anything tragic happened. It was a miracle that no one got hurt. I drove across the bridge, pulled over, and just sat in the car. That incident told me I had not been living right. I had weathered storms while aspiring higher and been blessed to achieve my own dream of playing in the NBA. But still, I wasn't getting the message. "This ain't right," I said. "I've got to change." And I did, as I sat there just off the Mississippi River Bridge. That incident led me to become a committed Christian. It was, literally and figuratively, my wake-up call. I didn't stop drinking altogether; I still enjoy a good wine at the proper time; but I am no longer a heavy, social drinker. More importantly, I decided that night just how I wanted to live my life. It was like the U2 song that goes, "I still haven't found what I'm looking for." That's how I felt before that night on the Mississippi River Bridge. But that night I did find what I was looking for. Before that, I was sick of me. I hadn't yet gotten to where I wanted to be as a man, and without a commitment to something bigger than myself, I never would. None of us will. From that night on, becoming a truly committed Christian was my goal. *Storm* lifted.

Making the team in Seattle was my basketball goal. When I achieved that in the fall of 1988 I felt joy and exhilaration. When I sprinted around that gym at the end of training camp, I felt like I was walking on clouds. My intent is not to sound arrogant but, looking back, I felt blessed. With my foundation in faith, and the recommitment to having a life based in faith following my rookie year, God blessed me, *spared me* on that bridge, kept me, delivered me, and protected me all those years. I know that with God's help I was able to play sixteen years in the league and manage it masterfully. I had to manage rejection. I had to manage being cut twice and traded twice. I had to manage loneliness; my family moved to Houston in 1991, and I spent many seasons away from my wife, Cassandra, and my children, Avery Jr. and Christianne. I had to manage women; every professional athlete does. I had to manage being married to my college sweetheart and *staying* married. I had to manage my teammates—some talented, some not—and I had to manage playing for thirteen different coaches in six different cities.

I had to manage an emergency illness. During the same off-season when I nearly ran my car off the Mississippi River Bridge, I also had emergency sinus surgery. My head was killing me throughout the season. A CAT scan one day found I had fluid in my sinuses eight inches from my brain. I was immediately admitted to the hospital for emergency surgery. They went in right above my nose and drained my sinuses. I was in the hospital for five days.

I had to manage getting my teeth knocked out by Lakers forward A.C. Green, one of the most outspoken Christian athletes ever. Not long after we'd just been in pregame chapel together, he knocked me across the mouth as I drove for the basket. It was not intentional—at least I don't think so! I was on Vicodin for two days.

I had to manage tragedy—the death of my father in October 1992, two months before our daughter was born. He died of a heart attack. In January of that year, I had signed with the Houston Rockets after weathering a storm of playing under two ten-day contracts before I made the team. That may have been the most pressure I faced in my entire playing career. The season before that the team won fifty-two games and head coach Don Chaney had been named Coach of the Year. But, the Rockets lost in the first round of the playoffs that season, the fifth straight year the team had lost in the opening round. The team struggled in 1991–92 the following season, and just one month after I signed on, Chaney was fired. He was replaced by Rudy Tomjanovich, the former Rocket forward who was then most famous for being the guy who survived the scary punch by Kermit Washington of the Los Angeles Lakers on December 9, 1977. I played in forty-nine games for the Rockets, averaging a respectable 3.4 assists in almost sixteen minutes as starting point guard Kenny Smith's backup. We didn't make the playoffs, but I thought I played well enough to solidify my position. Then came another storm.

In July that summer I went to Chicago to play in a charity game for Jesse Jackson's PUSH Excel organization. I woke up the next morning and read that the Rockets had signed Scotty Brooks, another backup point guard. I called Rudy to see what was up. He was brutally honest. "Avery, I never really liked your game," he said. "You're a great guy, but you can't shoot." I'd shot a respectable 47 percent that year, but I confess my outside shot was not great. It was not my strength—never had been. Teams played off me because they knew it was my weakness. I was still quick enough—and smart enough, due to hours of watching game films—to get around most defenders and find my way to the basket. But most coaches are locked into these images of what a player of a specific position is supposed to look like: what a center is supposed to look like, what a power forward is supposed to look like, and, of course, what a point guard is supposed to look like. They've locked in what type of skills he's supposed to have. Clearly, he's not supposed to be under six feet tall and have no J. That would be me. That was the season Kenny Smith (K.S.) worked with me on my jumper, and I thought I had made a lot of improvement. The spot on the floor in the arena that used to be called The Summit, where I took most of those jump shots with K.S., is now near where the altar sits for Joel Osteen's Lakewood Church. He bought the building, refurbished it, and now fills it every Sunday. I feel like I was warming it up for him.

After my chat with Rudy, I was scared: I was under contract
for the 1992–93 season, and was to earn $165,000—the most I'd
made so far. My fear was that I'd get cut too late in training
camp to get picked up by someone else, so I asked the Rockets to
cut me immediately so I could hook on with another team. They
refused to do it, though, so I held out of summer camp. I stayed
home to continue to try and get released. Imagine, a guy like
me—playing for near the league minimum with no one knock-
ing at my door—holding out. I must have been nuts. Or determined.

So there I was at home, not knowing anything about my
NBA future. I didn't know how we were going to pay our bills. I
didn't know much of anything. Then I got the call that Dad was
in the hospital. Cassandra and I flew home to New Orleans to
visit him. He was in intensive care, but he said he was feeling
fine. "Son, go back home," he told me. "I'll be okay." When we
got back to Houston I got the telephone call. He was gone. Suddenly, I really didn't care what happened to my basketball career. The man who taught me everything I knew about being a
man was gone, and it *hurt*. It hurt so much that I became angry
at the same God I had praised when I made the team in Seattle;
the same God I praised when I married my wife; the same God
I praised when I learned we would have a child; the same God
in whom I had unwavering faith. I was angry with my God for
months, until later that year when I became a parent and our
daughter was born. That event changed my life and made me
grateful to God again.

I was not grateful during those months after my dad died. I

was still scared. With no money coming in, we were basically broke. I was trying to pay for the house in New Orleans I'd bought for my mom. I'm not talking about a mansion, but it was another mortgage. I was trying to pay our bills in Houston; my wife, a nurse, was working twelve hours a day. Maybe she was tired on this particular day. She said to me: "Honey, enough. You have to get a real job. Maybe you're not good enough." I cannot convey in these pages just how much those words were a disappointment, coming from my wife.

My father was dead, my basketball career was maybe dead, too. It felt like God had abandoned me, and I wondered if Cassandra was right. I wondered if it was time to leave basketball behind. But I was still determined, just as I had been at every critical stage of my life. I took a stand and prayed that He was not ready for me to quit. Turns out, He wasn't.

Eric Musselman, who later coached the Golden State Warriors and the Sacramento Kings, was a young coach and general manager in Rapid City, South Dakota, home to a Continental Basketball Association team called the Thrillers. I didn't know him at all, but he offered me a contract to play for them. I even signed it; that's how determined I was to stay in the game. Even if it wasn't the NBA. But before I could get on the plane, the very same day I signed the Thrillers contract, Spurs general manager Bob Bass called and offered me a contract for $140,000. God had not abandoned me after all. Tested me? You got that right—but He did not abandon me, and He hasn't ever since.

Just because I signed a new contract doesn't mean the tests ended. The Spurs' head coach was Jerry Tarkanian, "Tark the

Shark," the towel-chewing former University of Nevada, Las Vegas, coach who won a national championship at the helm of the Running Rebels. Alas, he was not happy to see me. "You're not the guy I wanted," he told me. He wanted Gary Grant, who was still with the Los Angeles Clippers, the team that drafted him in the first round the same year I got out of college. "If you're that good," Tark said. "I don't understand how you can be out of an NBA job." *Storm.* Despite Tark's harsh words, I was pleasant and didn't want to cause any disruption, but once the season began he refused to play me. He wasn't mean to me; he just wouldn't play me. Two weeks after my arrival, just twenty games into the season, he was fired—another storm lifted. The new coach? John Lucas (or "Luke"), my former teammate and cab-buddy in Seattle. *Hallelujah!* On the first day of practice, Luke gathered the team together, pointed to me, and said, "Gentlemen, this is our starting point guard." He didn't focus on my weaknesses; he appreciated my strengths. There are no perfect point guards, no perfect players, coaches, bosses, teachers, executives, or entrepreneurs. People who seek perfection are destined to fall short of their aspirations, destined to fail. Those are the people who also fail to see the value of the positives in others. In many instances, they end up surpassed by those people they overlooked. As for Tark, a few years later he sent me a letter that was very complimentary. When I ran into him one day, long after our experience together, he said, "I would still be coaching today if I had not refused to play you."

Lucas played me and I was pretty much a starter for the rest of my career. Four years after Tark was fired, I finally got to play for Gregg Popovich ("Pop") when he was a head coach. In 1996–97, he was the Spurs' general manager. With the team struggling, he fired Bob Hill eighteen games into the season and named himself head coach. By then, I'd known him for years, and from the beginning of our relationship, he saw the positives in me. He did not see a poor outside shooter. He saw a great finisher around the basket. He saw a tremendous passer. He saw a leader who played with purpose but who was coachable and unselfish. He saw what I call *stretchability*—someone who has the ability to stretch others to become better players.

Popovich believed in practice too, and he taught me discipline and defense. In me, he saw someone who asked a lot of questions, and who sometimes questioned him, and he saw someone who didn't always vent the right way. Most of all, he saw that we could win together—even though he had never been a head coach at any level. In him, I saw discipline. I saw a defensive-minded guy who understood the importance of the details. He even had a particular way he wanted the ball passed into the big men on the post. I also saw a master delegator who trusted the men who worked for him. They weren't there to stab him in the back or take his job–they were all there for one purpose and with one mind—to win. Later, when I became a head coach, this was just one of the valuable lessons I took from Pop: to surround myself with the right kind of people.

Another coach who loved practice—loved, loved, loved practice—was Larry Brown, who I played for on the Spurs during the 1990–91 season. With Coach Brown, the key to success was practice, practice, practice. Today, we have player development coaches on our staffs who work with players individually on different skills. Larry Brown was the player development coach on our team—player development *and* head coach. He worked with me every single day. He worked with me on fundamentals. He worked with me on pivots and passing and shooting every single day. Every day when I got to the gym he was always already there.

Pop may have been disciplined but he was also positive. To endure and weather the storms, staying positive is key, though it may be the hardest thing to do. Why? Because we live in such a negative society. We are surrounded with negative talk—throughout the media and closer to home, among our friends and family. How are the highest-rated radio talk shows? Negative. Something is *always* wrong with America, the government, entertainers, pro athletes—everyone but themselves. I think a big reason for this negativity is that most people aren't really self-motivated and tend to possess low self-esteem. So they focus on the negatives of others—she's *too fat*, he's *not smart*, he's *not fast enough*, she's *not good enough*—in order to feel superior. Those same people also focus on not having enough. Others just hate themselves and never give themselves a chance to aspire higher. *I don't know if I can compete at that level.* They fail to determine and focus on what they do *well*: I'm a great organizer; I'm great at communicating; I'm energetic; I'm a forward thinker with great ideas; I get results. No matter the profession—whether advertising, technology, teaching, sports, media, manufacturing, finance, or cooking—everyone has been created with an attribute, a strength, a gift that can sustain them throughout their lives. You'll only find yours by being positive about yourself, particularly through the storms, and by refusing to accept the negatives hurled at you by others. Tuning out those negative thoughts is critical to turning a storm into a cool, comfortable breeze at your back. Negativism only feeds the storm.

The negativism that surrounded me as a young Black kid could have been devastating. More than anything, when I was eighteen and didn't know whether or not I was going to be able to go to college, I didn't want to be a statistic. I didn't want to be just another African-American man to end up in the criminal justice system rather than in college. I wanted to beat that. I wanted to beat the statistics that said White men stood double the chance of succeeding than Black men. I wanted to beat the statistic that said White men were less likely to live in poverty than Black men. I wanted to beat the statistic that said Black men were more likely to abandon their kids than any other group. A lot of other guys I played with throughout the years had more of a gift for basketball than I did, but they couldn't beat the statistics. I knew I could.

Imagine if I'd listened to every coach who told me I couldn't shoot or said I was too short. I heard them, but I did not accept that my weakness or height were enough to deter me from my goals. Instead I embraced my positives. I embraced my strengths: my ability to create assists—opportunities for others to score; my ability to watch hours of film and break down exactly what I needed to do to get past a defender; my ability to lead. That was my biggest positive and I'm still riding the hell out of it.

I've mentioned the importance of knowing how to delegate

and I want to talk more about that. Leadership is not only defined as the ability to persuade others to work on your behalf.
Great leaders also possess the ability to delegate. In order to
delegate, you must have smart, decisive, detailed-oriented *servants*. Yes, I said servants. Above all, the men and women you
entrust to execute your vision—whether on the playing field, in
the classroom, or in your company—are there to serve you, not
to take your job. Often leaders will hire a person for his or her
skills without assessing the extent of his or her *will* to serve. The
lack of willingness to serve is like kryptonite to higher aspirations.

With their intent to serve, those to whom you delegate must
have integrity, must be intuitive, and must be able to know how
to resolve issues. They must be good at conflict resolution. Then
they have to know how to interpret the information delegated to
them and illustrate it to their team so that it makes sense. That
can often take time, so they must also be patient. Successful im-
plementation of any vision—personal or corporate—cannot be
done impatiently. Instructions plus impatience equals incom-
plete results.

I first met Pop almost midway through the 1990–91 season
when I began my first stint with the Spurs after playing twenty-
one games in Denver. He was an assistant coach under Larry
Brown. He was a loyal servant. I think he saw positives in me
then, but he was not the head guy. The Spurs couldn't get out of
the second round under Brown and he was fired twenty games
into the season (along with his entire staff, including Pop) and
replaced by Bob Bass on an interim basis. At the end of the

1992–93 season, the Spurs didn't want to offer me a guaranteed contract despite the fact that I started forty-nine games and averaged 7.5 assists. We'd just lost to Phoenix in the second round of the playoffs and they thought Kevin Pritchard, a journeyman who's now the general manager of the Portland Trail Blazers, would do a better job as point guard. *Storm.*

My daughter was almost one year old. I was home in the fall, not knowing where or if I would play the following season, when I heard from Pop. After being fired by San Antonio, he joined Don Nelson as an assistant coach at Golden State. He said, "Get your bags packed because Tim Hardaway blew his knee out in preseason." The Warriors offered me $300,000 guaranteed, plus an option year—my option either to accept the second year or not. I signed in late October, just before the season opener. And, Nellie named me the starting point guard and captain. Once again, He had not abandoned me.

That 1993–94 squad was the best Warrior team in years— and the best Golden State team for a long time after. Chris Webber was our stud. Latrell Sprewell made the all-star team. Chris Mullin, a former all-star, was still playing well. It was quite a group. Webber was eighteen or nineteen years old, straight from his freshman year at Michigan where he was the leader of the famous "Fab Five" Wolverines. He was just two years from living with his momma, yet he was confident—very confident. As far as he was concerned, he was on top of the world. He was the first pick in the draft. He had great hands and was a great passer. He and Nellie didn't get along too well but he was a very skilled player. Mullin was a sharpshooting veteran. He was so cool, having grown up in Queens, sometimes we'd think he was a "brother." He was just a hip family man. Plus, he had also battled some of his own demons. By then, he'd been very public about his battle against alcoholism and was now sober. We got along, in part, because he and I had been down the same road. Then there was crazy Latrell Sprewell. I had so much fun with that guy. He was loud and very confident. He thought he was the baddest dude in the league. He was a fourth-quarter guy, one of the best clutch players I ever played with. We also had Keith "Mister" Jennings, a 5' 7" inch point guard. I was just glad to be taller than someone on my team; it hadn't happened in a while. Billy Owens was the smoothest guy on the team. He was quiet, but he could do it all. He was Nellie's point forward. A lot of the offense went through him. Off the bench we had Chris Gatling. He was our version of Vinnie Johnson of the Detroit Pistons, who everyone called the Microwave because he'd heat things up so quickly off the bench. Off the court we were a fun group. We had fun trips on the road, on the Champion Air charters that flew us around. Man, we had fun on that plane. And our home arena in Oakland was poppin'—just like it was again last season during our playoff series with the Warriors. We had the Raiders fans who needed something to do in the NFL's off-season. I started seventy games that year, and we reached the playoffs. We were good, just not as good as some of the other teams in the Western Conference. We were swept 3–0 by Phoenix in the first round. Still, that year was one of the most fun seasons I had in the NBA.

About a week after that season ended, Pop called me and once again said, "Pack your bags." He was heading back to San Antonio. He'd just been named vice president and general manager of the Spurs. "Turn down your option year," he said. "You're gonna be the point guard for the Spurs."

The following season, 1994–95, was as satisfying as a season could be without winning a title. As I've mentioned before, this was the best team I ever played for. We began the season 9–11, then won fifty-three of our next sixty-two games. It was astonishing. We finished 62–20. We had a *lot* of fun. Winning is fun; it dominates all storms. Although he was past his prime, Moses Malone (who'd won an NBA title with the Philadelphia 76ers and is one of the game's greatest centers ever) was still a force (if only for a few minutes at a time), and he was funny. One of my favorite Moses stories occurred when he was trying to tell David Robinson that he had to be more assertive, more demanding— more a "chief" than just an "Indian." "There can only be one chief," he was yelling in that big, deep Southern voice one day after practice. "When I was in Philly, I was the chief. The ball came to Mo. We had Doctor J [Julius Erving], Andrew Toney, Maurice Cheeks, but the ball came to Mo. Mo was chief. We got in trouble, the ball came to Mo." It wasn't eloquent, but, as usual, Moses made his point. Needless to say, everyone, including the coaches, was rolling with laughter.

I've already told you how Hakeem Olajuwon beat us in the Western Conference finals that year. He didn't beat David Robinson—he beat our entire team. He was on another planet that season and the Rockets went on to win their second straight NBA title. The funny thing is that Olajuwon was so good that everyone forgets that Drexler, the ten-time all-star guard, was also on that team, having been traded there by Portland. So were a couple of youngsters with promise: third-year forward Robert Horry and a confident young point guard named Sam Cassell, who was in his second season. In game one, Robert hit a timely, wide-open jumper to win the game because we didn't rotate to him. More than a decade later, Robert's known as "Big Shot Bob" because of all the huge shots he's hit in the playoffs during his career. Sometimes I think it's our fault: he hit his first "big shot" against us.

The following year, 1995–96, we lost to Utah, which was led by John Stockton and Karl Malone, four games to two in the second round of the playoffs. It was still a fun season, even with the disappointing ending. But 1996–97? *Storm.* It was a storm that led to Tim Duncan, but who knew at the time?

Our years of playoff losses had our head coach Bob Hill on the hot seat. Even though we won fifty-nine games in 1995–96, as I've mentioned, he was fired eighteen games into the follow-ing season and replaced by Pop. But the year got worse. I think I was the only one healthy the entire season. David Robinson played only six games after breaking his left foot, and Sean Elliott missed half the year with tendonitis in his right knee. The losing weighed on me; I was almost physically ill at times. The lowest low was walking into the gym almost every night and knowing you were going to get killed. Low was being ahead by fifteen points with five minutes to go and knowing you were still going to lose. We just didn't have the firepower that year to compete with good NBA teams. We barely had the firepower to compete with not-so-good NBA teams. That season became an evaluating year for the Spurs. Pop was evaluating a lot of talent. He had to think about the guys he wanted to invite back the next season, and who he didn't. Pop stopped playing me for awhile, for my own good, he said. Pop is more than a basketball coach; he's a life coach. "There's something positive that could come out of this," he used to say to me sometimes, even on the bench during the most dismal games.

None of us knew at the time that the good to come out of it was going to be Tim Duncan, the number-one pick in the 1997 draft. The Boston Celtics had two chances to win the lottery; we had one. They ended up with the number three and number six picks, which proved to be Chauncey Billups (whom they traded to Toronto before the end of his rookie season and who later became a star with the world champion Pistons), and Ron Mercer, who never really had an impact in the league. We got Tim.

As I already mentioned, Tim, a 6'11" forward/center, was great from day one. He and David found a way to make our Twin Towers lineup work. It worked because they were both unselfish. Alone, things didn't always work in David's favor, but sharing the floor with Tim, the young buck, put new pep in the Admiral's step, and he learned to pick his spots. David was smart enough to recognize soon after Tim arrived that the kid was special. He realized, *I don't have what this young guy has. I will help him grow.* Tim was a killer. He was ruthless. He may not talk loudly or a lot, but he was (is) an assassin. David realized that Tim could help him win a championship. By then, David had accomplished almost everything in basketball. A former No. 1 draft pick, he'd been the league's MVP, and he was the most important athlete in San Antonio history. David really elevated sports in San Antonio. He was the reason the Alamodome was built, he was the reason the AT&T Center was built, and he is the reason why all those hotels are still being built in San Antonio. It became a destination city because of David Robinson. He's the rock of the franchise. He's the rock of that city. Tim Duncan was the quiet killer, but David Robinson was the foundation. When you think of the Spurs you still think of David Robinson. Tim Duncan may have won more championships—four to David's two—but were it not for David Robinson, that town might have only known Tim Duncan in an opposing team's uniform.

We lost to Utah again in the playoffs during Tim's first season, and that summer I endured another storm. Cassandra and I went on vacation to Fisher Island near Miami. My mom had been battling cancer for a while; it was all over her body. But when we left her for our vacation, she was feeling good. We arrived in Miami and took the ferry to Fisher Island. We'd just unpacked our bags when one of my best friends, Barry Stamps, called and said he was at Mom's house with the emergency medical people and Mom was not breathing. They were trying to revive her, but the tone in his voice told me all I needed to know. Finally he said it: "She's gone." We immediately repacked and returned home. Both my parents were gone, but they had been true blessings in my life for as long as God needed them to be here.

If you're lucky as a player, you have a season like the one we had that following year, 1998–99. Everything came together. We had the right ingredients to be a championship contender *and* we made it happen. David became the leader everyone wanted him to be, but the burden of being the leading producer was shared with Tim, who began dominating the NBA like he did in college. Smooth, fundamentally sound, and committed, he just got it early—earlier than most young players. It didn't hurt to have David there for him, plus we had other leaders and producers, such as Mario Elie and Jerome Kersey—guys who'd been to the playoffs and knew what was required to survive— and Steve Kerr, who already had a championship ring.

Guiding that team was a joy. We rolled through the Western Conference, winning eleven of twelve games, then we wore down the New York Knicks four games to one in the Finals. I never in my wildest dreams thought I'd be in position to hit the winning shot in a championship game, but as I've said, God works in wondrous ways. He puts people in our lives who prepare us for the moments when we can deliver on the potential He puts in all of us. You just have to be open to them and aware of them. I worked and worked and worked until my shooting form was more structured and consistent so I'd be able to give myself a better chance to hit the outside shot. Then as I mentioned in the Introduction, Steve Kerr, who'd just joined the team that season, gave me the confidence I needed to be ready for the moment. *Just step up and knock it down.* Who are the people in your life who just might be preparing you for something greater later? They might be sitting next to you in the office and working on a project with you. They might be the older coworker offering sound advice. They might be a friend, your pastor, or a fellow church member giving counsel. The person might even be the boss you disdain, the troublesome employee, or the former business partner who let you down. Are you aware of them? More importantly, are you listening to them? If not, you might be missing the one key bit of data you need to achieve your own higher aspirations.

I thought I was going to retire as a Spur. But at the end of the 2000–01 season, after being swept by Kobe Bryant and the Los Angeles Lakers in the Western Conference finals, the Spurs told me they only had a slot that paid the minimum for veterans who played ten years or more in the league—$1 million. I know it's a lot of money, an amount I would never trivialize, but that season I'd earned $8 million, the most I had ever made in my career. I was thirty-six years old, I'd won an NBA title, and I'd earned more money than I could have dreamed. I was at peace. I was ready to step away and coach, something I had been preparing myself to do for years, maybe as far back as Southern. If you could ask my dad, he'd probably say even longer. But then the Denver Nuggets called with a whopper: three years and $15 million. Shoot, even my man Pop was stunned. "I'll help you pack," he said.

I thought I'd be in Denver for awhile, at least three years. That was my retirement plan. I even invested in a beautiful home in Castle Pines, one of the most exclusive communities in the area. However, one day in February, right around midseason,

I was taking Avery Jr. to get his hair cut when my agent called. "Pack your bags," he said. "Mark Cuban is at the Denver airport on his Gulfstream waiting to take you to Dallas. You've been traded." The deal was me, Raef LaFrentz, Nick Van Exel, and Tariq Abdul-Wahad for Juwan Howard, Donnell Harvey, Tim Hardaway, and a 2002 first-round pick. There were only seventeen games left in the season. When I told my wife, she started crying.

I wasn't completely happy either. At this point in my career, I knew I was a backup, but the Mavericks starting point guard, Steve Nash, was not one of my favorite people. Okay folks, don't get carried away. Steve is a great player, one of the best point guards of all time. A two-time MVP and still counting. But at the time, he was not one of my favorite people because we'd gotten into a minor squabble at the end of the game when I was with the Spurs and we were about to eliminate them in the first round of the 1991 playoffs, during his first stint with the Phoenix Suns. After the trade, everyone wanted to know how we were going to get along. Believe it or not, the relationship worked out great. Moreover, this was when Don Nelson was starting to work me into coaching for real. I always sat next to the coaches during games, and when Steve came off the floor, he sat next to me and I'd tell him what he was doing right and what he was doing wrong. Despite our squabble, he was always open to what I had to say. When Nellie gave me chances to coach the team during practices, Steve was always receptive. Steve didn't practice much, but on the days I coached practice he always joined the guys on the floor. Today we have a great relationship. He treats my son like his own and sends signed sneakers to my wife for her annual charity auction. Before games he waves to me. It's just an acknowledgment of respect and friendship. I feel I helped him get better.

My season and a half in Dallas was more of a beginning than an end. Playing under Nellie, I was often given the opportunity to run practices and make suggestions. I got an inside look at a team built to score but little else. In 2002–03, we torched our way through the schedule. We were described as "a 100-point game waiting to happen." We opened the season winning fourteen straight—one short of the NBA record—and finished 60–22. Dirk, Nash, and Michael Finley were almost unstoppable. We reached the Western Conference finals that season but lost to the Spurs after Dirk suffered a knee injury in game three. The series had been tied 1–1, but our depth was lacking and we could not overcome the loss of Dirk.

After the following season, in August 2003, the Mavericks tried to address their lack of depth with another monster trade—involving me again. I was sent to the Golden State Warriors along with Van Exel, Evan Eschmeyer, Popeye Jones, and Antoine Rigaudeau in exchange for Antawn Jamison, Chris Mills, Danny Fortson, and Jiri Welsch. I didn't want to go. I contemplated retiring rather than reporting to the Warriors. By then they had deteriorated and I did not want to go through another losing experience. But I went. I was not completely sure why at the time, but I later realized I had some personal coaching to do.

There was someone on that team who needed help, who needed someone to help him aspire higher. That guy was Jason Richardson, one of the Warriors' emerging young stars (more on our relationship in a later chapter).

As expected, we weren't very good and I missed my family back in Houston. It was not quite a storm; I'd been through so many at that juncture that playing on a losing team was not exactly misery. I was no longer the young boy from Southern, the kid who ran around the gym screaming in Seattle, or the one who struggled to prove himself every night, every day, every shot. By now I was a man, a veteran NBA starting point guard, and a champion. Nothing would ever take that away—nothing. It was just a rough year.

The following season, 2003–04, the Mavs brought me back as player/coach. But as you might recall, Devin Harris, a young point guard looking to get a couple of notches on his belt against an old vet, showed me very quickly that the "player" part of my new job was a bad idea.

And that's when I started the next part of my life's journey. Managing the in-between. From the day when I sprinted around the gym in Seattle because I'd made the team, to the day I told Mavericks owner Mark Cuban I no longer wanted to play, that's what I did: manage the in-between. How did I do it? I did it by following the advice I'm giving in this book, by paying attention to the key Ds: Determination, Discipline, and Decisions; by never losing faith and trusting in my loved ones and close colleagues. When you are in between—and we all are—you should try and never view what you do to earn a living as work. One of the things I've always tried to do is never say, "I'm going to work." Instead, I say, "I'm going to make a difference."

When you're trying to aspire higher, even during the storms, don't look at your job as work. Work never inspired anyone. Making a difference is not only inspiring, but also gratifying. My attitude is, "How many people can I help today?"

One of my good friends here in Dallas, Trevor Rees-Jones, was celebrated all across the city in 2006 after he sold his company, Chief Oil & Gas, for $2.63 billion, but hardly anyone mentioned the three major financial storms he endured before starting Chief Oil. How did he manage the in-between? How did he manage the experiences and relationships between his storms? How did he manage a sale that would land him at number 242 on *Forbes* magazine's list of the 400 Richest Americans? That's what I'm talking about. Managing the in-between.

Through the peaks, the valleys, and the storms, the charge for each of us is clear: manage the in-between.

Along the way it's important to have personal goals, but it is equally important to develop personal relationships with key people. I had a chance to work in the catering industry during the summer after my sophomore year at Cameron University. Another option was to work at Crescent Plywood for a gentleman you already know from the Decisions chapter, Mr. Norman Chenevert. The catering gig was physically the easiest, but my dad told me that if I went to work for Mr. Chenevert, "You'll never go broke again in your life." He knew how good Mr. Chenevert had been to him.

That was absolutely true. For years to come, every time I came home I dropped by his shop to say hello, and every time he gave me a folded one-hundred-dollar bill. To this day, I keep a crisp one-hundred-dollar bill in my wallet, and I've given hundreds of them away to young men and women who are aspiring higher and need a Norman Chenevert in their lives. Especially during the storms.

FIVE

A Strategy for Success: Standards

NOW THAT YOU POSSESS THE TOOLS to aspire higher, you need a strategy that enables you to wield those tools efficiently and effectively. Tools alone are not enough; in fact, they're worthless without quality materials and a sound strategy. Try building anything with cheap materials, or without a blueprint or a plan. Then they're just tools.

Similarly, talent isn't always enough. Every player in the NBA knows another player who was better than they were when they were kids, but that guy didn't make it. The reason had nothing to do with talent. The guys who didn't make it did not have a sound strategy of achieving their goal of playing pro ball. They had the tools, but that's all. For me, that guy was Dwayne Lewis. He was the best player on my high school team at St. Augustine. I thought at the time that he was one of the best players in the country. He could do it all. He was better than another teammate, Donald Royal, who was being recruited by Notre Dame and Louisiana State University (he went to Notre Dame), and who played eight seasons in the NBA with five different teams. Why didn't Dwayne make it? A lack of discipline certainly was a factor. Also, he didn't have the right strategy to succeed in college. His grades weren't good; he struggled to graduate from St. Augustine. He tried to play at a couple of junior colleges but it just didn't work out for him.

The sports adage—the best *team* wins—is proven true every year, every season. I've written that the most talented team I ever played for was the 1994–95 San Antonio Spurs. We were loaded at every starting position and our bench was deep. We had talent. We were physical at every position and were experienced at winning. Individually, we were experienced at winning. Many of my teammates had won championships while playing for other teams, but together we hadn't won a damn thing. That year, we won sixty-two games and were one of the favorites to win the title. When you're on a team with that much talent, you get to a point when you develop what I call "sincere confidence." You believe, in the depths of your bones, "We can't be beat." It's not a phony confidence; we truly felt we were unbeatable, even if we played badly. We thought our second team could beat twenty other teams. We had shooting, quickness, experience, and savvy. We could go with a big lineup or a small one. We were smart, we could scuffle, and we had some fighters. We lost twenty games and it amazed us that we even lost that many.

We crushed Denver in the first round and beat the Los Angeles Lakers four games to two in the Western conference semifinals. But in the conference finals, we ran into a better team, the Houston Rockets, a team led by a great player, Hakeem (the Dream) Olajuwon.

The Rockets beat us four games to two. More to the point, Olajuwon beat us, but in that series Houston was also the better *team*. Strategically, we were sound. Our plan was to play him straight up defensively (meaning we would not double-team him) with either David Robinson, who won league MVP that year, or Dennis Rodman. We wouldn't give them a lot of help and stay home on the shooters. We respected Hakeem but with that Rockets team it was "pick your poison": They had a young Sam Cassell, Kenny Smith, Clyde Drexler, and Mario Elie—all top-gun outside shooters. It's just that Olajuwon blew up our strategy. He averaged 35.3 points per game in the series, and was pretty much unstoppable. We were down 0–2, tied it 2–2, and came back to the brand-new Alamodome for game five. But Dream just wouldn't let up. He scored 42 points, and we lost 111–90. We were done.

No strategy is infallible. Sometimes you may have a very sound strategy, but you still may struggle. You can still hit a slump. But you've got to stay the course and keep your self-confidence high. It's all part of learning to deal with the struggle.

Even though the 1994–95 team had the most talent of any I played for, we still struggled. What was the best *team* I played for? Of course it was the 1998–99 Spurs that won the NBA title. We didn't have as much talent as the 1994–95 team, but we had better execution, and oh yeah, this time we had our own Dream: Tim Duncan.

Tools can build anything, but only with quality materials and a smart strategy will the structure be sound. Your tools for aspiring higher are determination, discipline, and decisions. You—now resilient and committed to striving through the storms— need the quality materials necessary to achieve your aspirations. Now, let's talk about strategy—a strategy for success.

STANDARDS

There is a bar representing the standard of behavior by which we all live our lives. Anything above it is acceptable behavior. They are the things we do that make us proud, that we would not be ashamed to talk about to anyone, including our family and other people we care about most of all. Transgressions below the bar simply won't be tolerated. They are against what we say we stand for. Oh, we all sometimes fall short of our standard, even those among us who try to walk by faith and abide by God's commandments. We fall, too. We all fall, but we hold onto the bar—our standards—and live by it the best we can.

The bar itself also represents something. It represents expectations. It represents what we expect of ourselves. It represents what we expect to achieve in our lives—both professionally and personally. How high we place this bar represents the heights to which we aspire. For many people, this bar is too low. It's so low they can reach it while sitting down. It's so low they can step over without stretching too far. For some people it's so low they can crawl over it. Between age twelve and my mid-teens, my bar was very low. When I was much younger, I was an all-star in basketball, baseball, and just about any sport I played. Yeah, I thought I was going to the NBA! But when I turned twelve years old, I stopped growing and suddenly I was no longer the best kid on *any* of my teams. My bar was low at that point in my life. Somewhere in there, I lost any real hope or desire to play in the NBA. I didn't even think about the NBA anymore. During my second year of college, at Cameron, I was pretty low again. I was sitting on the bench, not playing at all. That was a down period for me socially, academically, and athletically. That was a very rough year—until I made one telephone call. I called my high school coach, who got me into Southern University.

During those years, I had a real battle going on in my sub-conscious. *What did I want to do with my life?* It affected my self-image and my self-worth. Your self-image will help you set the standards in your own life, and as you aspire higher it's important to become comfortable with where you *are* before you can be excited about where you are trying to go. It's important because that subconscious feeling never really leaves you—it goes to work with you, it comes home with you, it tucks you in at night. When bad things happen, the natural instinct is to react negatively, to get down on yourself and allow your self-image to slide. A low self-image can cloud your picture of who you want to be and where you *believe* you can go. It helps shape your direction and your vision. A poor self-image diminishes you—like breathing polluted air instead of fresh air every day. My environment at New Mexico JC and Cameron contributed to my low self-image. Southern lifted me and allowed me to set new standards for my life.

Ultimately, no one sets the level of your bar—your standards—but you. No one sets the level of my bar but me. As a child it was different. Like most of you (the lucky ones), I had parents who set my bars. They told me—and showed me—what was acceptable behavior at home, at church, with others, anywhere. Anything below that bar was unacceptable and, though it may not be allowed today, my butt was torn up when I did anything that was below the bar. As for the bar of expectations, they set that one high too. My father expected great things from me, not mediocrity. When I was about twelve years old, my dad and I were riding together. I was having a great day with my dad. We went to lunch after baseball practice and I was excited to be with him. At one point I turned to him and said, "Dad, I want to be just like you." Within a half-second he slapped me—hard, right in the mouth. "To me," he said, "that's mediocrity. I'm a man with a sixth-grade education. I want you to be *ten times better* than me." I don't advocate the slapping; I was hurt at the time, but later I understood what he was saying. "I'm not the standard," he was saying, "the standard is higher." He made his point and I never forgot that.

How high is your bar? How much do you expect of yourself? What are your standards of behavior? What will you tolerate of yourself—and others? Professionally, how high are your current aspirations? What do you expect to achieve? The answers to all of these questions represent your current barometer—where you are now. Then, very simply, you must raise your bar. Raise your standards of behavior and expectations. If you are going to go higher, then there must be a new bar, one you quickly become committed to exceeding. Your new mentality must be: *This is my standard, this is my bar. I must operate above this standard. I cannot settle for anything below it.*

Standards change. My bar was almost always high, my standards were always higher than most of my friends, my classmates, and even my relatives. Only one person in my family—my older brother, Andre—had gone to college. But I was going, too, and I was going to get my degree. As a matter of fact, I was going to get my master's. High bar; high standard. In high school, my basketball standard was initially low. Because I was one of the last guys on the bench, I just wanted to *play*. Once I got the opportunity to play at the end of my senior season, I wanted to play *in college*. That was a pretty high bar for someone who was not recruited at all. Once I arrived at New Mexico JC and played, I wanted to play for a *bigger college:* higher bar. After I saw Southern play against St. John's in the NCAA tournament, *I* wanted to play in the *NCAA tournament:* higher bar. Once I showed at Southern that I could play on that level—and play well at that level—I wanted to play in the *NBA:* very high bar. And once I got to the pros, I told myself, Hey, I want to be a *starter:* extremely high bar. Being an NBA starter was my perception of success because as a starter I would make enough money to solve a lot of my family's financial problems. After that, I wanted to be *a coach.* When setting higher standards, remember that they should be accomplished with appropriate steps, none of which should be skipped.

Today my bar remains high. I want to be a *better* coach, a *great* coach, an *NBA championship* coach. I want to be a better husband and father, a better friend, a better listener. I want to be a better boss, a better Christian. By continuing to raise your standard, you are stretching yourself. Having high standards stretches us. Simply by reading this book you're showing that you want to be stretched. You don't want to be stagnant. You want to be smarter, to be better. I want people to see the difference in my standards. I want my kids to see me being a better father. I want my wife to see me being a better husband. I want people who do not even know me personally to see me being a better Christian man every day. How others see me is important to me. I want to see the change in my bar and I'm not going to see a change unless I am stretched.

When you are stretching yourself, always operate in a state of excellence. For me, that means I want everything I do to be first class. I don't want it to be mediocre. I want to be a high-performance person. I want to be a model for others who wish to raise their standard. As you aspire toward new goals, make being an example for others part of your new standards. You really have no choice; aspiring higher will put you in the spotlight. Guaranteed. I want to be excellent at solving problems. That's what I get paid to do. Coaching is solving problems—on the court, and off. People are watching. As you try to reach higher, people will be watching to see how you handle yourself. They want to see how you handle success and setbacks, how you handle getting

the promotion or getting fired, how you handle a financial setback or prosperity. They want to see how you handle your employer. In the spotlight, they want to see how you handle the
thrill of victory and, especially, agony of defeat.

My bar was high. My standards were high. They still are.
And yet I could have easily fallen short. I could have been in-
jured. I might not have been invited to an NBA camp, or I
might have been invited by a team that did not need a small
point guard, or by one whose coaches focused on my bad jump
shot rather than my playmaking skills. I could have also fallen
short on my new standards of behavior. I could have practiced
less and slept more. I could have settled for being in less than
the best physical condition. I could have continued being a social alcoholic. A lot of things could have happened to prevent me
from staying above the higher standards of behavior I established for myself, and from achieving the high standards of
achievement I set for myself. But they didn't.

However, you don't want to have a standard so high it leads
to frustration. Then it becomes all but unachievable. Now that
you know your gifts, now that you've got the tools to succeed and
you've eliminated the losers and naysayers from your life, you
should have a realistic sense of what you can achieve if you make
the commitment and raise your standards. Determine those
standards and goals—then raise them just a bit higher. Raise
your standards high enough that you know it will require a lot
of work and effort to get there. Make your standards high, but
reachable. And though your bar is high, you must have a realistic
understanding of the timing required to reach the new standard.

You must understand timing. You must understand minutes. You must understand seconds. You must understand hours, days, months, and years. I've mentioned before that we live in a "microwave" era when people expect things instantly. But real success has no timetable. Most successful people understand that. It takes as long as it takes. If you just graduated from law school, why set your bar at being a partner in a year? I wanted to be a head coach. My standard was for it to happen three years after I became an assistant coach. It came sooner than I thought—in six months—but I didn't say I *had* to get it in six months. It was a blessing that it happened that quickly, but my timetable was more realistic.

I understood the concept of being seasoned. I knew that in order to reach my standards I had to become seasoned. I needed time to grow. You have high standards, but don't forget that you may need to become seasoned in order to achieve them.

How quickly I became a head coach throws off other former players. They look at it externally, as if I went straight from playing to being a head coach and that becomes the standard they set for themselves. A lot of people thought I became a head coach overnight. Oh, no. They don't understand I was being seasoned to be a coach throughout the second half of my playing career. I helped to design drills. I watched film after my teammates went home. I watched film like a coach, and I spoke like a coach. I was named to the league's all-interview team for three years. If you look back at my interviews, you'll see that I was speaking *coach*, so not only were others speaking about me as a coach, I was speaking it about me. I was very specific about what I wanted to do. A lot of players say they'll never go into coaching after their career, but maybe after some failed businesses or a lot of time doing almost nothing, they might discover they're almost forty years old and nothing gives them as much joy as the game of basketball. Being a head coach might then become their new standard, but many of them are not willing to be seasoned.

I get tons of calls from former NBA players who want to coach. They want to do it like I did and go straight from the locker room to the sideline as a first assistant. They don't want to hear anything about coaching in the Continental Basketball Association or working as a scout. They've raised the bar, which is a good thing, but they've raised it without embracing the determination, discipline, and decisions necessary to reach it. They raised it without a sound and realistic strategy for achieving their goal. How do you determine just how high to raise your bar, how high to set your standards? That will be partly determined by what you've been exposed to throughout your life. A lot of what I've become as a player, a coach, and a man is not just because of who raised me, or the environment I grew up in, but because of what I've been exposed to in my days since leaving New Orleans for New Mexico JC and beyond.

And once your bar is set, you have to leverage all your experiences and assets in order to reach it. Sometimes you might need a friend or colleague to help you see that you're not doing enough. For example, I was once on a plane and I asked the flight attendant for some hot tea. She brought me the tea, but it was cold. I asked her if she would warm it up. You'd have thought

I asked her to do 100 push-ups. She brought the warm tea to me, but it came with a bad attitude. I then asked her for some sugar. You'd have thought I asked her to do 200 push-ups this time! Throughout the rest of the flight I got bad service with a bad attitude.

Because I'd traveled all over the world and been exposed to other airlines with better service, I knew she could do better. I knew she should have done better. As I got off the plane, I told another flight attendant that she needed to give her colleague a crash course on what it means to be a flight attendant. She needed to show her how high the bar is for real flight attendants.

As you might guess, I cannot tolerate bad service. In a restaurant, in a store, anywhere—I understand what it means to provide good, professional service and I will not tolerate anything less. I hate being in a store and standing there forever before someone asks you if you need help. I understand standards. I have high standards for myself and expect others to have high standards for themselves as well. Nothing less should be acceptable.

I've also been around players with all sorts of standards. Some only worked hard enough to keep getting paid, barely hard enough. Others worked hard morning, noon, and night— constantly improving on all aspects of their game, including their fundamentals. They all had different standards and, not surprisingly, they pretty much all had levels of success in accordance with those standards. The most frustrating guys for me were those whose main focus was just on getting paid. I heard that so much during my career. There weren't many who said, "I want to make a difference. I want to get paid so I can make a difference or do something significant in my community." Nope, their focus was just on getting paid. That was their standard. It was frustrating. I wanted to get paid to give scholarships to kids, to give hope to kids who have no hope. I wanted to get paid to help single mothers. I've done all that throughout my career. I wanted to get paid so I could make a difference.

Just know this when you decide to raise your standards: Easy doesn't do it. Raising your standards to a place that's easy to achieve is not really raising your standards. Just as you don't want to raise the bar too high, there's nothing gained by keeping it too low, either. There's nothing to gain but maybe becoming one of those "treadmill people" I wrote about; someone who just runs in place and goes nowhere. That's easy. That is not aspiring higher.

Another aspect of raising your standards is leadership. Raising the bar for yourself gives you an opportunity to develop your leadership potential. In truth, leadership is an obligation for anyone with high standards and aspirations. When you raise the bar on your personal expectations, others expect more of you, as well. And when it comes to the requirements of leadership, I think of the six Cs: competence, character, class, cooperation, caring, and communication.

Of course, leadership requires *competence*. Leaders are expected to lead by doing. Whatever the challenge, the leader is expected to show the way. One reason I stay in shape—I work out an hour before every game and regularly during the off-season—is that I sometimes have to show my players what I want them to do. I have to get out on the court during practice and demonstrate the play. I have to show them how to play defense, how to guard someone, where they have to be on the court when we're in a particular defense. I believe the players respect a coach more when he can get in the mix and show them how it's done. Competence.

Leadership also requires *character* and *class*. How many leaders—supposed leaders—were undone in recent years because they failed to show high character and class? So many CEOs have been brought down by greed or behavior that did not meet the standards of their position. Even in sports, leaders—coaches and players—have been compromised by their lack of character and class, both on and especially off the playing field. Competence alone might help you achieve a leadership position, but you will not keep it without displaying character and class. And you can't be complacent. Not in any capacity. Whether you're a corporate manager, the superintendent of schools, the mayor, or a local real estate developer, complacency cannot be part of your strategy.

Leaders must also *cooperate.* Some people achieve new levels of success and suddenly they believe they're the smartest person in the room and don't want to cooperate with anyone. Being the Mavericks head coach is not about Avery Johnson; it's about the Mavericks. There are a lot of social functions that may not be the most convenient for me to attend—I may be tired from a long road trip, for instance—but I cooperate because it's about the franchise, not me. It's the same with my players. They don't always agree with everything I say but they have to cooperate.

The next critical "C" required for leadership is that you have to *care* about more than yourself. Specifically, leaders must care about those they are leading and demonstrate a true compassion for them. Leadership without caring and compassion is a dictatorship and they rarely sustain any success they might achieve. In basketball, players can tell when the coach doesn't truly care about them, either about their improvement or what's going on in their lives. Some coaches are all about winning, but the best coaches are those who coach both to win the game and for the players to win in their own lives. I was blessed to play for coaches and general managers throughout most of my career who I felt genuinely cared about me. Not all of them, mind you, but the ones I've written about here all did, and that made a big difference to me. It also made a big difference to my teammates that they felt the coach cared about more than whether they hit the shot when time expired or whether they executed the defense correctly. Those things matter in the short run but what matters more in the long run when you are trying to aspire higher is caring.

Leaders must also be able to *communicate*—both verbally and nonverbally. Verbally, it's important to communicate positively to individuals who you work with or who are in your circle of support. Tell them you appreciate them. Tell them you need them. Tell them they did a good job, and to keep working hard. Tough communication is sometimes just as necessary, though. *You were late. You need to come to work earlier. I need you to work harder.* After I've delivered bad news I usually try to soften it a bit with some nonverbal communication. I might leave them a gift card for a local music store. Sometimes I'll take them to dinner, send them flowers, a restaurant gift certificate, or a movie gift card. These are all forms of communication that say, *I care about you.* Most of all, in the end honesty always wins.

Competence, character, class, cooperation, caring, and communication. Think about the people in your life who've been leaders, either at home, at work, or at church. Some have done well in a few areas, but were lacking in others. They might have been competent, but not of strong character. They might have been caring but not competent. They might have had character but were not able to communicate. Some people get to be leaders without some of those qualities, but consider the ones who are the best leaders, the ones with the longest tenures and the most loyal followers. Consider the ones who influenced you most. Think of the ones you most want to emulate. Chances are, they exhibited each of those characteristics: all of them.

When I became head coach of the Mavericks in 2005, the team's standard was simple: *Let's outscore our opponent.* I tried to raise the bar. I told the team: Yes, let's outscore them, but let's become *defensive-minded.* Let's start thinking defensively. Let's breathe it in, and make it part of our mind-set. Let's show other teams we are as passionate about the defensive end as the offensive end. We will outscore them *and* stop them from scoring. That should be our standard.

I had to change the standard on how we played defense, how we practiced. Initially we spent much more time working on defense than offense. Scoring was almost natural to this group, whereas defense was work. It was not instinctual, so we had to spend more time on it until it started to sink in and become part of our DNA.

We were not going to be able to compete for a championship until we became defensive-minded. We weren't going to be perceived as true contenders until we became defensive-minded. I knew that from my days with the Spurs: we didn't become defensive-minded until Pop took over during the 1996–97 season. All he talked about was defense. *We've got to play defense like Detroit.* That year training camp was the hardest of my career. Every drill we did was a defensive drill. Did we embrace it? I know I didn't. Pop used to tell me I was the worst defensive point guard in the league. But I was pretty tough-minded. I knew I wasn't the *worst* defensive point guard in the league.

The Mavs haven't quite yet become the playoff defensive-minded team that I want us to be. We're still working on that, still aspiring. Of course we had to make some changes. Some of the players embraced the new standard, while others didn't. The ones who didn't had to go. We brought in players we felt would bring their own defensive-mindedness to the team: centers Erick Dampier and DeSagana Diop, along with Adrian Griffin, Brendan Bain, Eddie Jones, Devean George, and Trenton Hassell. We need those guys to be defensive guys. We also need them to push and complement the guys who carry us offensively. And we need everyone to be *strong.*

Sometimes in your own business, you have to make changes. As you raise the standards, some will be able to reach it, others will not. That's real. In basketball, new players bring their experiences—what they've been exposed to—to your team, your environment. New employees bring what they've been exposed to. It's a risk, and sometimes you just don't know. A lot of people can talk themselves into a job but when they get there you discover they cannot meet your standards.

When I was younger I wanted to set standards for my own siblings. I wanted to raise the bar on how my younger sister viewed college. My attending Southern inspired her to go to college, at Dillard University, and now she's an accountant for the judicial system in New Orleans. My niece, Tanya, was inspired to go to LSU and now she's a chiropractor. My wife, Cassandra, inspired her own sister to aspire higher. My wife raised the standard, and worked hard to become a nurse. She took her certification test three times, never losing her determination. Now her sister's a nurse, as well.

The struggle with standards comes when you have to fire somebody. I don't like to fire anybody. I struggle with that. I hate final-cut day before the regular season starts. I don't like to be the bearer of bad news. I don't like to say: *We no longer need your services; we've waived you.* I don't mind trading a player, but I don't like waiving them. I got waived twice myself, so I know how it feels, and it doesn't feel good. The first time I got cut I didn't even know what being 'cut' meant. I was playing for Denver, or at least I was wearing a Nuggets uniform. I wasn't playing at all. The coach was Paul Westhead and Bernie Bickerstaff, my first coach in Seattle, was the general manager. We were in Portland after a game when the coach calls me into his office. We'd just lost and I didn't play, so I thought he was calling me in to say he was going to play me more. Instead he said, "We're cutting you." I didn't know what that meant. I was thinking, "Cut what? My playing time? You can't cut that because I'm not playing. So what are you talking about?" When he told me what being "cut" meant, I was wiped out, stunned. I got back to the hotel and called my fianceé (now my wife). She was crushed. Then I had to fly back to Denver with the team—on the same plane. It was surreal. Everyone else was laughing and joking around and I just sat there in shock. I didn't know what I would do. Once I got back to Denver, I packed up and went home to New Orleans for Christmas.

Something inside me didn't give up, though. Today, I think of the saying: The eagle has the vision, the bird sees. There's a big difference. The responsibility of the visionary—the eagle— is to set the standard. If you want to aspire higher sometimes it is all about knowing when to raise your standards—or even when to lower them. Yes, lower them. Sometimes you may have to go lower for a moment in order to raise the bar later.

Maybe you're in a 1,500-square-foot house and you have no problem handling the mortgage payments. You want a 3,000-square-foot home that would obviously cost more, but can't afford the higher payment. You see another home that's 2,200 square feet. You really want more space, but this one won't put a financial strain on your wallet. You can also continue to save your money and come back in a few years for the larger home. So you lower the bar temporarily. The right decision gets you to a better place financially so you can come back later and meet the new higher bar you originally envisioned.

Sometimes you set the standard too high and you lose sight of the foundation needed to reach it. Last season, for instance, in 2006–07, we got caught up in winning games and maybe lost sight of our goal—winning a championship. We didn't talk about it, but I have a sense that winning seventy games—something only one team had ever accomplished in NBA history—became our unspoken standard. And it took a lot of energy. It became an exterior standard—one imposed by circumstances or other forces—but it manifested itself internally. It became our standard even if we didn't want to admit it.

What are your standards? How low are they? How high do you want to aspire? Are your current standards, in every aspect of your life, high enough to get you there? If not, make the decision today to raise the bar.

SIX

Systems

ONCE YOU'VE RAISED YOUR STANDARDS, how do you reach them? How do you become the person you aspire to be? For starters, you'll need to assess your *system.* What current behaviors and attitudes do you possess that are preventing you from meeting your new standards? What behaviors and attitudes are you lacking that are necessary if you're going to achieve your goals? Once you've answered those questions, you'll probably need to create a new system designed to give you the best opportunity to achieve your goals. In short, you'll need a plan.

Even though the Mavericks players quickly bought into our

new standard—being a defensive-minded team designed to win championships rather than an offensive-minded team designed to win games—they could not just get up the next morning, come to practice, and start doing things differently. They needed a plan. They needed someone to tell them how to make the transformation. They needed a step-by-step guide that outlined new behaviors designed to achieve the new goals. They almost needed to relearn the game of basketball from top to bottom.

Oh, they could still play. This was no doubt one of the most talented teams in the league. But they had to redirect their physical talent and, most importantly, their effort, to the defensive end of the floor. More than anything, our guys needed to take Defense 101. They needed to relearn the proper technique in all phases of defense. They needed to relearn one-on-one defensive techniques, how to play off the ball, and how to react within the "team defense" scheme. They needed to learn how to be in the right position on the floor. Then they had to learn the *mentality* of being defensive-minded. They had to make a commitment to being as dominant on the defensive end of the floor as they were explosive on the offensive end. They needed a plan.

For starters, our old way of practicing was too focused on offense and the "small picture" (winning games), not the "big picture" (winning a championship). But changing our mind-set was not going to be an overnight process. Creating your new system will also call for a self-assessment. Setting new standards is simple. You could probably sit down tomorrow and come up with a list of new goals, new standards. They are like New Year's resolutions. They look good—on paper. But they're not worth that paper if you don't make some essential changes in your life, if you don't implement a new system designed to *put you in position* to achieve your new standards.

Is your higher aspiration to lose twenty pounds before summer? It won't happen unless you change your diet and start to exercise regularly. Those are two elements of your new system, your new plan.

Is your higher aspiration to start your own business? It won't happen unless you begin learning as much as you can about entrepreneurs—both successful and unsuccessful—and incorporating their lessons into your own mentality. That's the beginning of your new system, your new plan.

Is your higher aspiration to become a model, or a dancer, or an artist, or an athlete? It won't happen until you shed all of the people from your life who doubt you—some of whom might even be family or your best friends—and surround yourself with positive people who are willing to help you become what you want to be.

Sometimes, systems are simple. A friend of mine who's in the oil business says when he started his company, his system wasn't really much of a system at all: "I wasn't necessarily smart enough to implement a system," he says. "All I knew was that I was going to persevere until it worked. To make money, you must have a mind-set that insists you are going to persevere. I didn't have a lot of fancy equipment or a lot of expertise at the time. I was going to keep drilling them oil wells until I found one of them suckers. I told the Lord, 'I just need *one*.' If I went broke, that was okay. Not much of a system, eh?"

Eventually he realized that perseverance alone wasn't enough—he needed a real system. He decided to base his plan on talent; in his case, other people's talents. This outside talent was going to help him reach his standard (striking oil) more efficiently. If you are an employer or an entrepreneur, you also are going to need good talent. You may have had the idea for the business, and you might even have the money, but those alone aren't enough. At some point you'll need other people to help you or you'll go broke. You need talent that is not only *skilled*, but talent that can be motivated or, in my world, coachable. Like me, you need talent that can *score*. Although we wanted to become a defensive-minded basketball team, at some point we've got to score. You must have people on your team who can score.

My friend in the oil business eventually had the kind of team that helped him become smarter about drilling. "Now we go into the pits and look at the land. We study the land to find out if the dirt is just dirt—'cause the money ain't in the land, it ain't in the dirt, it's in the minerals."

He remembers watching me as a player and says my system at that time wasn't very complicated, either. "Your system wasn't about making jump shots or getting assists," he told me. "Your system was perseverance. You played like the only thing on your mind was: 'I'm going to make it in the NBA.' You knew you had the skill level. You knew you had the talent. You just needed to persevere. I knew how to make it in the oil business. I just needed to persevere until I could get the talent I needed in order to win."

Another friend of mine, who is the CEO of a major dairy

company, also firmly believes that any system must be driven by talent—talent that can make you better, and can help you raise the standard. "Surround yourself with people you can learn from, people who can motivate *you*," he told me. "And if you're an employee, the best thing you can do to boost your own aspirations is to work for someone who can motivate you. If you're not around someone who can motivate you—who you respect, who you have confidence in—then, well, nothing works."

A system is a well-thought-out and organized plan. But no system will achieve the standard without talent. If you're looking for another job, don't just think about the particular title you want, think about the company itself. Ask yourself: Where do I want to work? Why do I want to work there? The next time you're interviewing for a job, ask yourself, Can this person inspire me to raise my standard? *Can they score?*

Ask yourself that same question if you're recruiting someone for your team, if you're hiring someone. Can they score? Are they self-motivated? Are they coachable? I want defensive-minded players because it takes defense to win championships, but I don't want players who are always on the defensive. I need people who can score. When creating and implementing a system, you want people who can score. You want people who go south and can make things go north. You want people who can shake things up. You want people who know how to respond when they—or the team—are under pressure.

Your system must be built on your own commitment to *perseverance*. And it must include *people* who motivate you. But listen to me now: Your system also must be *patient*. Too often we look at patience as punishment. Some of us say we're patient but what we really have is impatient patience—we might be patient for a few weeks or a few months, but at some point we lose our patience and end up scrapping the system because we think it isn't working. Sometimes it doesn't. Sometimes you need a new plan. More often than not, though, you simply need more patience. Change takes time. Rather, *effective* change takes time. Like me, you want to make change happen, and you want it to happen *now*. But change for the sake of change is not good enough. It's just, well, change.

If you want to reach a higher level in your corporation and you know all of the executives at that level have MBAs, then it's pretty clear you'll likely have to obtain one, too. Getting a master's degree in any field isn't easy, and obtaining one requires sacrifice. It requires time, money, and a laserlike focus. Patience.

Someone in business might want to become an investment broker. Doing so requires passing the Series 7 and Series 66 exams, which are long, detailed, and dense. Can you set aside your social life, friends, and maybe even your family long enough to study for and pass the tests? Patience.

Quitting smoking may be one of the most valuable high aspirations anyone can pursue. But ask someone who's done it how easy it was. Better yet, ask someone who has tried and failed. How intensely do you aspire toward a healthier life? Patience.

Being a better parent means attending more parent–teacher conferences, asking about your child's homework every night, attending more plays and sporting events, and maybe just sitting down more and asking your child what's on his or her mind. It may seem easy, but for many parents—those focused more on making money or enjoying themselves socially—these changes are difficult and they require patience.

There are many NBA teams that would like to perform better defensively, but for various reasons it just doesn't happen. Sometimes it's the people. Any player can play defense, but not every player *will* play defense. Sometimes it's a lack of perseverance. Devising an effective strategy, and then executing it, requires an all-out commitment to endure the rough patches when the strategy doesn't seem to be working. And, of course, that means patience must be embraced by players and coaches—and even the fans.

Here's another ingredient required for any system; one that, when lacking, can render all the others null and void: *preparation*. In implementing our new system I began with a simple premise, one that should be a cornerstone of your own new system: I needed to prepare my players by putting them in the right *position* to play defense. They needed to be in the right position on the court. They needed to have better footwork. They needed to know a proper defensive stance. They needed to know where to watch a player when playing defense against him. And they needed to know how to react to their man's offensive moves. They had to be in the right position before they could be effective they had to be prepared.

Get yourself in the right position to succeed. You must be in the right place, not the wrong place. You've got to be prepared physically and mentally. Lazy and unfocused won't do. And you've got to be committed to maintaining the right position even as others try to force you to compromise it. Being out of position—even slightly—can have a profoundly negative effect on your result.

For someone aspiring to lose weight, the right positions are in the gym and at the salad bar. The wrong positions are at the refrigerator or in the fast-food drive-through lane.

For someone aspiring to become a screenwriter, the right position is in a writing-for-television course where you can learn the craft of writing dialogue, scenes, and plots. The wrong position is simply in front of the television watching shows.

For someone aspiring to become a chef, the right positions are in the kitchen and as an apprentice in a restaurant. The wrong position is just sitting at the table.

To ensure we were in the right position defensively I had to reposition our players mentally—off and on the court. I had to reorganize our practices to place more emphasis on defense, spending more time on defensive drills. I had to educate the players about where to be on the court in different situations. I had to educate them on how and when to react to the offensive player so that the defensive tactic is most effective. Heck, I had to start with showing them the proper defensive stance. Then, after they got the "what," I had to work on the "why." I had to inform and challenge them mentally to make our new defensive-minded system work.

Information is another bedrock of your new system. Anyone who aspires higher must, in addition to using the tools and strategies outlined in the previous pages—be armed with the right information. Remember when you had to write a research paper in school? Did you just start writing, making up facts as you went? No, you did your research first. You got the facts, figures, dates, and names of the important people. You got the information. When you want to start a new business, do you just hang a shingle and open the doors? No, you do research. You look at businesses like the one you'd like to launch. You research their start-up costs, expenses, and potential revenue. You check out locations. You look at the marketplace: the competition and the customer base. You study their mistakes, as well as the smart decisions they made. You get the information.

Another friend of mine owns a General Motors dealership. When he first bought the business he wanted to raise the standard and sell more cars. He knew he needed a new system in order to achieve that standard, but in order to create that system he needed fresh information: How effective were the billboards surrounding the dealership, and did he have to change them? How important were financing and service plans to customers, and did he need to devise some more creative options? Should he create giveaways to draw people into the dealership? Were his print ads as effective as they needed to be to increase traffic through the doors? What about radio or local cable television ads? Should he appear in the ads or should he hire a pretty model? Should he require everyone on his sales team to carry not only business cards but also DVDs and brochures about the dealership? He needed to research answers for all of these questions and more, before he devised an effective strategy. Information.

Information for my defensive strategy was gained from my

experiences with other teams, particularly San Antonio. Defense was our priority there. Sure, we worked on our offensive sets and strategies for different situations. We worked on them over and over until we got it right. But defense: that was our bread-and-butter. That was our rock, our weapon. We knew we won more games with the big defensive stop than we could with the big shot. Offense can be fleeting. Defense, when played with the proper positioning and level of passion, is steady, solid, and strong. But the Mavs weren't the Spurs. Our strengths were different. Our *people* were different. But we could still find our own way.

I began by restructuring practices. Before I became head coach, maybe 35 percent of practice was spent on defensive drills—and little of that with intense effort—so we dedicated at least half of each practice to defensive drills, and not half-heartedly, either. There were more *teaching* defensive drills: some focused on technique (the crouched stance, keeping arms and head up, keeping eyes focused), some emphasizing positioning on the court and technique (how to force a guy toward one direction or another, how to play a shooter versus an opponent who is a threat to dribble around you, how to be physical without committing fouls, how to play the passing lane). We watched more defensive film, and we watched it differently. We asked guys to study the players they'd be covering, to study them with more purpose than they did before. On some days it must have seemed like we *only* played defense. But that was all right. As coaches we had to demonstrate just how important it was to us before it would become important to the players.

A key to teaching the Mavs to be as aggressive on defense as they were on offense was to devise a system that prepared them to play that way during games. They needed a new mind-set that said: *This game will be won on the defensive end of the floor, not on offense.* Too often, especially in the fourth quarter of a tight game, players resort to what's comfortable rather than what's necessary, which might be harder. Defense is hard, and it's certainly not comfortable. Playing defensive-minded basketball requires a commitment some teams just aren't willing to make.

When I began to incorporate defense into our team philosophy, for some of our players this new system was a stretch. They had never before been asked to make such a commitment to defense. Those who hung in there with me, however, will tell you that their patience has paid off. They just had to get through the bumps of learning something new. They had to break down that wall, and trust that I knew what I was talking about.

The entire system wasn't corrupt. I had to figure out which elements needed to be eliminated and which ones needed to be retained. I liked the way we played offense and ran the ball. I liked the way we played to our offensive strengths: the pick-and-roll and dribble penetration. We were confident and competent in those areas. But I didn't like our movement. We were too stagnant; too much one-on-one and not enough motion to keep our opponent off balance. We were scoring a lot of points, so it was easy to think our offensive system was solid. But we scored most of our points in transition—on the fast break or immediately thereafter before the defense could set up—but on a night when teams were able to slow down our break, we had trouble getting open shots. The perception was that we were explosive when the reality was that we could be diffused. That was not going to be part of my system. It was only through this process of analysis (from our researched information) that we were able to recognize our strengths and weaknesses and address them.

Once you have all the information, you must then use that information to analyze where you are and where you are going. You need to analyze who you are. You must determine if you need to restructure your system and, if so, if the changes should be big or small. I didn't want to display impatient patience and make radical changes, so I analyzed my people and made changes to reflect who we were. I restructured how we played certain defenses, how we played the pick-and-roll. Some strategies and systems, while they may have worked for another team, simply didn't work for us. I recognized that and made changes without scrapping the overall system.

When trying to raise the standard as the new CEO of an underperforming company, or a manager in an underperforming division, you will likely find that something is wrong with the system, but maybe not the whole system. The source of the trouble may be the accounting department, sales, or public relations. So you must look at how each of those departments is structured in order to assess if one or more of them should be changed. Sometimes the source of the breakdown is the people that are in position, not the system itself.

But sometimes it is actually the system. A friend of mine recently took over a business and after a few months, people still ask him: Did you clean house? Did you bring in your own people? His response was, "It wasn't the people; it was the system. Essentially, there was no system—at least not an effective one. So before I could evaluate the people, I had to create a system that was more efficient. I had to outline to the staff the higher standards I wanted for the company before I could determine if the people currently in position could reach the new bar." Turns out most of the people embraced the higher standard and accepted the challenge to follow the new system. A few didn't and resigned. As it says in the Bible, God moved them "to their own divine good." My friend says God knew what He was doing. The people who resigned would have probably been fired anyway. God indeed works in mysterious ways.

For anyone who is taking on a new, higher level of responsibility at a company, whether as CEO, regional executive, or a manager, the fundamental challenge is to assess the system and, if it's broken, determine why and what needs to be done. The same is true for any individual who has not been able to achieve the higher aspirations they may have set for themselves long ago. Determine why and what needs to be done.

If you're struggling to reach your goals—whether that goal is developing a new skill, getting a promotion, finding a new job, or improving your marriage—chances are something is wrong with your system. Ideally, a husband and wife will have a system for living, forgiving, and communicating. Too often, at least one of the three areas is not functioning properly (and in some instances, none of them are). When that happens it skews the system such that the marriage ceases to function. Living means embracing the spiritual concept of two people becoming one—one being, one mind, and one body in accord. Not every day, of course! But being of one accord means the creation of one new "life" from two. Forgiving is as vital as air because no marriage can thrive and survive without it. Communication is an every-day, every-hour, every-minute, every-second necessity—like oil in a car engine. It's the only system that works. It may not ensure that all of the parts run smoothly but without it a marriage is certain to fail.

The personal system that helps you reach your new standard might include more sleep, better nutritional habits, spending more time studying and reading—any number of things that create a focused model for success. It might take a while to define your new system, and there will almost certainly be some—probably a lot of—trial and error. Once you've found the right system, you might discover that implementing it—living it—requires a new *you* altogether.

If that's the case, once again you'll have to take an honest account of yourself and decide whether you truly want to commit to the new system. If you're not sure, revisit the standard and determine whether it's too steep. How high are you aspiring and is it realistic? If not, reevaluate and reassess where you'd like to be. Sometimes an "interim" standard is enough to start you on your way to the higher standard you ultimately want to achieve. If you want to run your own magazine, maybe it's best to set an interim standard, such as becoming an editor at an established magazine where you can learn the various elements of the job by observing the top editor and asking him or her questions that will better prepare you to run your own ship.

Without such an interim standard, you're more likely to make the mistakes that could have been avoided had you had more experience and preparation. Had I not sought out coaches while still a player and picked their brains for techniques and strategies, had I not taken on the opportunity to run practices while still a player, I may have easily failed when I became head coach of the Mavs with eighteen games left in the 2004–05 season. With those interim standards reached, I was better prepared. I trusted my skills and my instincts. And, just as important, my players trusted me.

Now I was able to implement the next step in my system, and it's a critical step for any system. I call it recruit and incorporate, and it pertains to the "people" element I discussed earlier in this chapter. Recruit partners for your system. These are people who *enable* your system, not *disable* it. They are the people who have your back when you need a lift, rather than being potential backstabbers who want what you have. Just as you need to eliminate the people in your life who operate beneath your standard—and thus threaten to drag you beneath where you aspire to be—you have to incorporate people into your circle who will become the threads of your support system.

You cannot aspire higher alone. Your standards may be your own, but your system has to be a partnership, not a dictatorship. The people you recruit must stay true to your fundamental *principles,* but while they support your ideas, goals, and principles, they are also a great source of new ideas and strategies. Be open to them. If someone has a better way, then listen. Be open-minded. They are your "teammates."

In my practices, or even in games, if a player has a better idea, a better strategy, or a better option, I'll say: "Let's do it that way." There's no room for ego or arrogance when you have high aspirations. No successful person ever accomplished anything alone. They had some type of support group: a spouse or partner, a mentor, a family member, a peer, a friend, a close co-worker. Chances are they were part of a team, one built on a system with high standards.

I'm all about partnerships. In our system, teammates and coaches are partners, and partnerships lead to trust. In fact, our system is based on trust. I tell the players: You've got to trust your teammates and the coaching staff, and we must trust you. You must have confidence that you can carry your teammate when he needs a lift. You must have his back, and he must have yours, anywhere on the court. And if one of the coaches or players says anything to help achieve that, they are teaching me—not being critical of me—because he wants me to get better. In our system, teammates and coaches are partners.

In any company, from the smallest mom-and-pop to the top of the Fortune 500, employees should have an ownership stake. Ownership is empowerment; it's validation of the partnership. In major companies, the ownership stake is often in the form of stock options. Smaller companies may not have those perks, so employees in those companies must feel as if they have an ownership stake in the *ideas* that drive the company's success. They must believe that the person in charge values their opinions. If they believe that you believe in them, they'll tend to go the extra mile for you, for the company. And that is in your best interests.

I won't win an NBA championship as a coach unless my players embrace the standards and the system I've implemented—and then deliver! You won't achieve your goals unless your team does the same, whether it is comprised of the employees in your firm, your family, or the support system you've built to encourage your personal ambitions. You can't win without them, so they should have a stake in the victory.

There are times during games when what I want is not working. It's just not working. That's when possibly a player, or one of my assistant coaches, will recommend a different course of action, a different tactic. I'll always listen, and then I'll make the call. That kind of across-the-board empowerment and sharing of ideas is in our culture. The entire Mavs organization tries to give different people the opportunity to offer ideas on things throughout the company, even when it comes to how our home games can be more entertaining. I get feedback from our families and players throughout the year, and we share that with our arena. Partnership.

Any effective system has to be inflexible in some areas. We're not flexible when it comes to rebounding. We're not flexible when it comes to being on time. We're not flexible on attending weight-training sessions (something we're putting more emphasis on this season). We're not flexible on our standards of behavior on the road. Those standards cannot be compromised.

I was very blessed in my playing career to be exposed to different coaches. It helped expose me to several systems that, ultimately, I didn't want to be part of my own system. I saw a lot of what I did not like, a lot of practice techniques and relationships with players that were not conducive to getting the best out of the player, and so they were not conducive to winning. On the other hand, I learned various things from different coaches' techniques that I did want to incorporate into my system. I learned discipline from Gregg Popovich. I learned unique offensive techniques from Don Nelson. Bernie Bickerstaff showed me how to handle a young basketball team, particularly young African-American players. He accepted that we were not ready to compete for a title, so he helped us to become better professionals. I mentioned before that Larry Brown was the best practice coach. He was more passionate about the practices than games. He was always teaching. Popovich was also a defensive guy. Both he and Larry were awesome at handling great players. They allowed their best players to be their most important partners and allowed them to set the standards that the rest of the team followed. Bob Hill was extremely organized on the bench during games. He has a great system for keeping every kind of statistic you can imagine, and then making it easy to access during games. He also introduced me to extensive film study. John Lucas emphasized fitness and working out like no other coach I played for. He designed prepractice and off-season workouts. There was weight training and flexibility. He believed conditioning made it easier to keep following the system as the body began to tire. Luke was all about fitness.

I incorporated all of their strengths into my system. We have young players and we have superstars. We can always become better professionals. We have organized practices and my coaches all have specific statistical responsibilities during games. Three seasons ago we hired an assistant trainer from the NFL, Dionne Calhoun. He used to work for the San Francisco 49ers, and I'm hoping he—along with our head trainer, Casey Smith—will add some of that NFL toughness to our team. If we wanted to compete for an NBA championship, we had to evaluate our system and implement one that would help us achieve that goal, and we did that by utilizing perseverance, people, preparation, and patient patience as the bedrocks of our system. We recruited "partners" (players and coaches or, for you, employees and people in your support system), and incorporated information gained from research and experience into our new system. None of these elements function without the other.

If you want to aspire higher, do you think your current system is enough? If not, make sure your system is worthy of your standards. Make sure it's a *winning-minded* system.

SEVEN

Take a Stand

AT SOME POINT IN YOUR JOURNEY higher, you will come to a crossroads—a place where you will be asked to make a critical decision. Your strategy is working. You've established new standards, and your system is keeping you focused on your goals and aspirations. Then something happens. Perhaps a coworker will attempt to convince you that there's no reason to check the numbers on tomorrow's report one more time. Perhaps you're a bit tired, so you're considering skipping today's workout. Maybe you're a student thinking that tonight's class just isn't that important. Maybe that extra hour of practice at the piano you promised yourself is not such a big deal. You figure you don't need to do that extra bit of work. You've worked hard already and you'll be fine, right? Wrong. You won't be fine. Take a stand.

The numbers in the report are fine. Well, maybe they aren't. Take a stand; check them again. You'll still look good and be healthy without today's workout, so take the day off. That may be true for today, sure, but not if skipping workouts becomes a habit. Take a stand. Get to the gym. You'll just get the notes from a classmate and you'll still ace the assignment. No, you won't. Take a stand. Get to class.

Another hour of practice won't make much difference, and you'll still hit all the notes at that recital. No, you won't. Take a stand. Practice.

If everything you've read up to now in this book can be characterized as nouns and pronouns, this chapter is the *verb*. It's time for action, time to take a stand. You're almost there. You're well on your way toward realizing your dream. Aspiring higher still isn't easy. You're still dealing with doubts and challenges and nothing is guaranteed, but you feel good about your progress. You've weathered some storms. You've been committed to success and you're confident you'll achieve it. Now, there's no surrender. Not now. You're on the front line of the journey and there's no retreat.

I call it being "sold out" to the goals. You believe what you believe. You believe in yourself. You believe in your close family and friends. You believe in your faith. You're prepared to reach higher. You're unequivocal and uncompromising about what it takes to accomplish the goal. You're excited and passionate about the future. Bring it on!

You're sold out on yourself!

Right now, I'm sold out on our commitment to winning a championship. I'm sold out on what I believe it takes to achieve that goal—the kind of behavior, work habits, and discipline— and I'm not willing to diminish those beliefs. I have a certain way I like to practice, a certain way I like to *prepare* for practice. Most days when we're in Dallas, I'm in the office early. Sometimes I never leave; I sleep there (on days when I'm not in the office early, I'm taking my kids to school). One of the first things I do is to jot down a list of ideas I have for that day's practice. I've looked at films of previous practices to see what we've done well and what we might need to work on. I've looked at the "practice notebooks" I've kept since I became a head coach. When my coaches begin to arrive I share my ideas with them and pick their brains for other ideas. Then I take all of that information and outline my practice for the day. My assistant types it up and makes copies, then I share it with the coaches. I will not compromise on that pattern and preparation. I've taken a stand that this is how we will do it with the Mavericks.

I'm not a big zone-defense guy. I think zones are a cop-out. I think bad defensive teams play zone. But I took a stand that I'd be open to the idea of a zone defense that I could be comfortable with. I took a stand, came up with a zone that works for us, and gave in to the idea. We worked on it and worked on it at practices, and it's actually helped us win some games. I'm still not a zone guy, but I do like to win games.

You should not compromise in your standards and systems. Take a stand on those principles and make it clear—to yourself and others—that this is how it should and must and will be done.

Perhaps you've implemented standards and systems for your children. You've implemented social standards regarding which other kids they can play or hang out with, and for how long. Maybe there is a curfew or a specific geographic area outside of which they cannot go without your permission. Maybe you've implemented academic standards about grades, homework, and class behavior. You've implemented athletic standards about which sports they can play and how diligent they have to be about attending practices. At some point you may have to take a stand because your child will want to play with someone you don't approve of, or they'll slack off in their study habits, or they'll start wanting to skip a practice. They may even want to quit. They may show signs that they'd be okay settling for mediocrity. Take a stand and make sure they know that's not how it should or will be done. Mediocrity, in any area of your life, cannot be acceptable if aspiring higher is the goal for you, your family, and your professional dreams.

My kids have heard me say this many times: *That is not acceptable.* Taking a stand is saying you're not going to accept what might be acceptable to others. You're not going to accept sub-par performance or behavior. Sometimes, my children will make a particular grade on a test, one they know I won't be happy with, and they'll say, "Well Daddy, I made a 70 but everybody else made a 65." My thought? A 70 is not the best they can do. So I've got to take a stand and say, "I don't care what everybody else in the class did. I don't even care if everyone else made 90. For you, 70 is still not acceptable—not because of how it measures against what the other kids did, but because it's not the best you can do. I'm measuring you against *you*."

When I was a kid, I used to ask my daddy if I could stay out as long as my friend, Kevin. My dad used to say I had to be home "before the street light came on" at the Lafitte Projects where we lived. Kevin's dad allowed him to stay out later. I used to get teased all the time by my friends because I couldn't stay out as long as the other kids. But my dad took a stand and said, "You'd better get your butt in here before the street lights come on." Thank God my daddy took a stand; Kevin ended up in jail.

Taking a stand doesn't always mean being inflexible. Remember my "stand" on zone defense? I took a stand instead to be open-minded. But on some things, well, you just have to stand solid. For instance, I take a stand on this one: No kids should wear their pants below their butt. There's nothing good being represented there. It represents prison culture. That's where the "style" began. Why would we celebrate an institution that has all but eliminated a generation of Black men and still lures too many of our young men and women? I'm taking a stand on that now. You're not going to change my mind on that one; no way. Avery Jr. is twelve years old and he's heard that a thousand times.

In basketball, there's no way you can make me believe that coming to practice late is acceptable. I take a stand on that one, too. My players have heard that one a thousand times. Being late is unacceptable, and my guys know it, so it rarely happens around here. But when it does I take a different approach than most coaches. You can fine players, you can make them run extra, but I play on their emotions. I'll say: "How could you have done that?" "How could you be so selfish and irresponsible?" "Being late is being a loser." "Champions aren't late, champions are early." "Would your mother want you to be late?" (That one really gets them.) "Who do you really care about? Do you think they'd want you to be late?" Then I might hit them with the entire weight of history. "There were people who paved the way for you to be here, who didn't make 5 percent of what you make. Do you think Oscar Robertson was late? Do you think Julius Erving was late? Do you think Jerry West was late, or Larry Bird?" Basically, I throw my psychology degree at them. And by the time I'm finished they wish they'd only been fined.

Take a stand for excellence. If you're working in a corporate environment but aspire to do work for yourself someday, take a stand for excellence. Take a stand that reports can't be late. Take a stand that your clients will always be satisfied. Take a stand that your sales numbers will always be at the top of the list. Take a stand to absorb every bit of knowledge possible from that environment so you'll avoid making mistakes when the business is your own. My coauthor is an editor and a writer. Missing a deadline is unacceptable to him. He takes a stand on that for himself and his staff. Whatever your vocation, take a stand. If you're a teacher, take a stand that no student will leave your class without knowing as much as he or she can know. Take a stand to make learning fun, and that they'll leave your class at the end of the school year more excited about learning than they were at the start of the year. If you're a doctor, take a stand that your patients will leave your office feeling as if they've received the very best care possible. If you're a real estate developer, take a stand that the buyers who invested their lifes' savings into the homes you built will live in a well-constructed place built with the highest-quality materials. If you're a mortgage lender take a stand that your clients are getting a good mortgage with reasonable terms—one they can actually afford, not one that might lead to foreclosure down the line. If you're a leader in your church, take a stand that members and visitors will leave each Sunday feeling warm, welcomed, and fulfilled with the Word.

Take a stand to be your best *you*.

Take a stand for yourself, especially when things aren't going well, when your efforts get derailed or become stagnant, as they invariably will. At times like these, it's easy to start feeling sorry for yourself. When your situation takes a downward turn, it's easy to doubt yourself and question whether your efforts are worth the hassle, all the determination, discipline, and decisions. Instead, say to yourself (out loud if you have to!): I'm going to hang in there. I'm going to *survive* this. I'm going to have a fighting spirit. I'm going to battle this setback. I'm going to stand strong.

That was my only choice in January of 1992 when, after being cut by the Spurs just before Christmas, I was signed to a ten-day contract by the Houston Rockets. In my mind, this was my last shot. If I didn't get signed for the rest of the 1991–92 season, I wasn't sure if I'd ever get back in the league. Teams are only permitted to sign players to two consecutive ten-day deals; after that the player must be signed for the remainder of the year or not signed at all. Playing in the NBA Finals a few years later was easier than playing on my second ten-day contract. That was the most pressure I felt during my career.

Throughout the first ten-day contract, all you're worried about is getting another ten-day deal, but when you're on the second ten-day, you feel like you're under a microscope. You're under a microscope every time you're in the game. You're under a microscope sitting on the bench. You're under a microscope riding on the bus. You're under a microscope in the locker room. You're under a microscope at practice. You're under a microscope at shoot-arounds on game mornings. You're under a microscope when the coach says hello, or doesn't say hello. You're under a microscope when you go to the bathroom, when you're in the shower. You feel like you're on pins and needles 24/7. In the second-to-last game on my second ten-day, I scored twenty-one points off the bench, and hit a big three-pointer from the left corner against the Minnesota Timberwolves. I thought that was going to seal it, but after the game, head coach Don Chaney said he still didn't know if I'd done enough. "I can't convince them," he told me. The next game was against Michael Jordan and the Chicago Bulls. I was in the game for the last possession. Coach was giving me every chance to show I deserved to stay, and I really appreciate that now. I remember my teammate, Vernon Maxwell, was all over Michael, talking crazy to him. Michael missed the shot and we won the game. I don't recall the score, only that we won and that I was in at the end. That night was the longest of my life. I was staying at the Renaissance Hotel right across the street from The Summit, where we played, but I didn't get much sleep. A lot of my teammates were supporting me. Kenny Smith kept saying, "You're on the team, man. You're on the team." I didn't get the call I was waiting for until early the next morning. It was Carroll Dawson, an assistant coach who later became the team's general manager. "We signed you for the rest of the year," he said. That was a real high, just like when I learned I'd made the team in Seattle as a rookie. That time I ran around the gym hollering like a little kid. This time, I thanked God. Ironically, Coach Chaney, the guy who fought hard for me, got fired a couple of weeks later.

Throughout that second ten-day contract, my whole mind-set was: *I'm making this team.* I had to work hard. I had to watch film. I could not be overwhelmed by nerves or anxiety. I couldn't allow setbacks like missed shots and turnovers deflate me. I couldn't let not playing many minutes deflate me. I had to take a stand and keep my wits about me. Funny thing is, seven years later, during the first half of game five of the 1998–99 NBA Finals, I had six turnovers in the first half. It was one of the worst halves in my career. But at halftime, my mind filled with memories of the pressure of playing under that second ten-day contract and how I took a stand on making the team; this helped calm me for the second half when I didn't have a single turnover.

You may also have to take a stand in the midst of prosperity. You may have to take a stand in the sunshine. Is everybody telling you how great you are at the office? Take a stand against complacency. People love your business plan; they say it's a "can't-miss" proposition. Take a stand against naïveté. Take a stand against ego. You just got a promotion and a raise. Take a stand against unnecessary spending. You just took your company public and the IPO made you an overnight millionaire. Take a stand for *humility*. Don't be prideful or arrogant. Don't believe the hype; believe you're *not* as good as everybody says you are (which, of course, means that if things turn against you, you're not as bad as they say you are, either). What I'm saying is to know that the source of your success isn't you. You achieved it with the help of others, or maybe you got a bit of a break somewhere along the way; there's nothing wrong with that. There were others along the way who helped you get to where you are, so don't be arrogant or prideful in your success.

My list of "others" is long and varied. Some names you'd recognize, but many you won't—like Joe "Squeak" Armant. I was about ten years old and playing at the local playground when this man I didn't know walked up to me. He said he was starting a Biddy Ball team—little kids playing basketball—at the local recreation center and he thought I'd benefit from it. I didn't know there were organized basketball teams in the area and I certainly didn't know him. "I need to talk to your dad," he said. "I'd like to tell him about this team." I went home and told my dad about this guy who was "bothering me" at the playground. Obviously he went down there. He met Mr. Armant, liked what he was saying, and enrolled me on the team at the Treme Recreation Center. Mr. Armant sought me out and gave me a break. He's just one of many. I am not here by myself.

Last season, as we were reeling off win after win, as we were striving toward sixty-seven wins, the most in the history of the Mavericks franchise, perhaps our biggest challenge was not believing we were as good as everyone was saying we were. Our success was real. Our success was fun. But really, it was just *perceived* success. Maybe each of us got caught up in it just a bit; after all, we're human. Real success would have been winning the championship, which didn't happen. Losing in the first round was hard, period. When people ask me whether being eliminated so early was devastating, I say losing—period—was hard. Would we have felt any better if we'd lost in the second round? No. Losing is losing and it never feels good.

This season, we're taking a stand to remain focused on winning a championship. That, and nothing else, is our purpose each day. There will be victories and setbacks along the way. But our vision is fixed on the long-term goal, nothing less. That was our mind-set from the opening day of training camp and it will remain our mind-set through our final game. That is our stand.

In the summer of 2000, when I was still playing, I took a stand on humility when I signed a contract worth $8 million for one season. It was toward the end of my time with the San Antonio Spurs, and it was two years after we'd won the NBA championship, so the new deal was a bit of a reward for my time there. Don't get me wrong; I celebrated (oh yes, I did). But I also stayed humble (and was humbled some more at the end of the season when the Spurs didn't re-sign me.)

I stayed humble by remembering how we were basically broke in 1990 after being cut by the Denver Nuggets just before Christmas, while my wife Cassandra was pregnant with Christianne, our first child. I stayed humble because I had many family members making only $8 an hour; I still do. I stayed humble by remembering the guys who had blown out their knees and knowing, but for the grace of God, how that could have been me. I stayed humble by recalling my years at New Mexico Junior College and Cameron University when I wondered whether I'd have to give up the game. I stayed humble by remembering how hard my dad worked, despite numerous heart attacks, and the fact that he died before I was financially able to do for him all that I'd wanted to do. I stayed humble because I watched a lot of different shows on Christian television networks in which various ministries were trying to raise, say, $30 a month to feed hungry kids in another country. That was pretty humbling.

When I won the league's sportsmanship award in 1998, when I hit the game-winning shot to win the NBA championship the following season, when I was named the 2006 Coach of the Year at the end of my first full season as a head coach, when we won sixty-seven games last season—they were all humbling experiences for this little kid from the Lafitte housing projects in New Orleans.

Take a stand that you will remain grounded through the peaks as well as the valleys, through the successes and the setbacks, through the fanfare and the failure—take a stand to remain *you*.

Taking a stand doesn't mean being irrational. I can take a stand and say the Mavs are going to be a great three-point shooting team. But what if we aren't constructed that way? I can take a stand and say we're going to win seventy games, but only one team in the history of the NBA has won that many games.

Moreover, winning seventy games is not *our standard*. Winning a championship is. You can take any stand you wish, but it may not fit. It may not be realistic. If it's even just 1 percent not the right thing for you to do, leave the door open and be rational about your decision.

Aspiring higher is stressful. It's stressful because it's easier to accept less than you're capable of than it is to stretch toward your best. It's stressful because as you rise, so do expectations. It's stressful mentally and physically. Take a stand to manage the stress you will inevitably encounter.

One of the ways I manage stress is to pray so that I won't become *prey*—prey to money, success, working abusive hours, losses, outsiders and their expectations, temptation, depression, others' opinions, food, a poisonous environment. I pray. I meditate. I pray that I won't allow the world to eat me up or deflate my spirit. I pray in the morning and often at night. I even pray during the day. Sometimes I just need to close the door to my office. Sometimes I just need to go for a walk. There's nothing like taking a stand with God.

As I'm sure you know by now, I've experienced some pretty stressful situations—in basketball and in life. I had to take a stand in the wake of Hurricane Katrina. I took a stand to do as much as I could for as many people as I could, but through it all I felt like I couldn't do enough. I was trying to get family members out of there and to our home in Houston. I was trying to get friends out of trouble. I was trying to send money all over the South. But it was never enough and there was so much I was powerless to do.

I couldn't reach some of my family members for several days. Some became homeless. Our home in Houston was like a command center. We put up anyone who made it to Houston and I called friends in Dallas to help those I knew who made it there. Cassandra wired money to relatives who found their way to other cities. It was around my fortieth birthday and my wife was going to throw a party. Instead, we hosted a fund-raiser for the victims of the hurricane.

My biggest fear involved my sister Cheryl, her husband, Rudy, and their daughter, Katera. They were trapped upstairs in their duplex apartment in New Orleans as Katrina's waters rose beneath them. After they retreated to the attic, Cheryl used her dying cell phone to call our brother, Cleveland, who had evacuated to Baton Rouge. "Lord Jesus," Cheryl prayed, "Are we going to get out of here?"

I felt helpless. I thought helpless was calling a play from the bench and depending on your players to run it, but this was very different. It was three days before rescuers paddled up to the attic window and pulled Cheryl and everyone else to safety. Other family members spent several nights in the Superdome and were eventually bused to Little Rock, Arkansas. When she got there, Cheryl borrowed a cell phone and sent me a text message that simply said, "Safe."

All that time, I was angry because the levees that were supposed to protect my hometown had been faulty since before I was born, and yet no one did a thing about it; not one thing. People in that city were living in the bottom of a big bowl, and everyone knew it. My mom used to talk about Hurricane Betsy, which struck New Orleans in 1965, the year I was born. At the time, it was the costliest hurricane in U.S. history. In fact, it caused over a billion dollars in damages. They even called it "Billion Dollar Betsy." But not a thing was done. As I tried to help, I grew angrier. I was angry at the government and angry because I couldn't get people out. I was angry as I watched all the people living (barely) in the Superdome. I was angry watching people dying in the streets. I couldn't believe what I was seeing. It was like watching a disaster in a Third World country, but this was my city and these were my people. I saw the streets where I went to school, where I went to church, where I went to the mall—and I couldn't do anything. I couldn't rent an airplane and go pick people up. Even with all my wealth, I felt helpless to help people. That was an extremely stressful time for me.

But I took a stand to be hopeful for my city, to be uplifting for the people there. Last summer I returned home and visited the Lafitte Projects where I grew up. To get off the bus and see it—well, it was like a ghost town. There was no sign of life. The place is boarded up while various government agencies fight over whether it can be reopened because so many people still need a place to live.

While there, I could see and hear the noises from my childhood. I could see people playing football in what we called The Court, which was just a field in between the buildings in the projects. I could see kids playing baseball. Behind one of the houses was a basketball court, and I could hear a ball bouncing and kids screaming. I could see and hear people walking around trying to sell me some praline candy. The experience kind of broke my heart because all that life was gone. I couldn't really see or hear anything, just ghosts.

The house where I grew up—605 North Miro—was boarded up. I could see the same air conditioning unit in the window. I could see the window where my room was in the back. Sometimes I used to sneak down the fire escape, go to parties, and sneak back into my room. I could visualize my daddy sitting on the porch smoking a Winston and drinking a Teacher's scotch after a long day. I could smell my Mom's food. I could see Dad's 1976 Chevy Impala. I could see it but I couldn't see it. It was very emotional. Ghosts.

I visited my high school, St. Augustine, and spoke to a group of students there. I told them they were "champions under construction," so they could feel confident about the control they have over their lives in an area where it might seem like they have no hope. I told them not to be afraid to take a stand for themselves.

As a coach, I've taken a stand regarding how I want us to play. As I mentioned in a previous chapter, I raised the standard for us defensively. I wanted us to be defensive-minded and accept nothing less. I wanted us to aspire toward winning a championship and accept nothing less. I pulled the best elements from some of the coaches I played for and created a system that would allow us to reach those standards. Now, my stand on Mavs basketball encompasses how we develop our game plans, how we practice, how coaches and players communicate to each other, and how we handle challenges.

Take a stand in your own life. Take a stand in your business based on a formula for success, a stand on how to increase sales, improve customer service, or create a better product. Take a stand and let it work.

You're going to be tested. You're going to be hit from behind by unexpected occurrences and by individuals who want to keep you on their level—individuals who want to keep you lower. You're going to be questioned on why and how and when. You will hear, *Well, it was done this way before you came along.* But you've got to be sold out to your vision and strategy. I took over the team with eighteen games before the end of the 2004–05 season. We went 16–2 and lost to the Phoenix Suns in the second round of the playoffs. I felt my players were pretty much sold out to the vision by the end of that year. I was convinced once everyone returned for training camp the following season. There was a different focus and attitude. Most importantly, we'd had some success with our higher standards and our new system. Now we needed to take a stand. Our run to the Finals was the direct result of everyone being sold out to the vision and taking a stand that we were not going to waver from our mission. We didn't win the title, which was our goal, but we had a great season and we left it being recommitted to the vision.

Taking a stand means you'll have a bunker mentality—you, the people you love and trust, and your mission are all in it together. You'll be sold out and committed to the vision through it all. You've got to feel like you're in it to win it today and tomorrow. You're just in it. You just will not be moved.

There may be better teams and better situations for me. Maybe there are better players on other teams. But I'm doing what I think is best for me and my family. There's always the possibility of something being better—a better job, a better city, a better boss, a better husband, or even a better child. There's always something better. But you know what? Sometimes you have to take a stand and be happy where you are.

For years when I was a player, the media talked about how the Spurs would never win a championship with me starting as point guard. *The Spurs need a point guard. Our point guard can't shoot.* I got so sick of hearing it. I got tired of defending myself. But Pop—Gregg Popovich—was sold out to me. That's why I was sold out to him. Finally, I had to take a stand. I said publicly that I'm the man for the job. Pop said it, too. Sometimes, taking a stand is a matter of putting it on your lips. Life is in the power of the tongue. Talk your stand. Take your stand.

EIGHT

Savor the Journey

ONE OF MY GOALS IN WRITING this book was to reach those whom I call the "in between" people. Some of them are people who have achieved something in their lives already. They've gone higher than they might have even expected of themselves, but they want to go even higher still. They're successful by most anyone's measure, but in their minds there's more to do. They're not done. Ask them and they say: *Hey, I'm just getting started.* Maybe they need to be more disciplined or consistent in order to reach higher. Maybe they need to be smarter. Maybe they need to be more focused. Maybe they need to be more confident. Maybe they need to discover their real "gift."

Let's face it: that's most of us. I'm in between. As a head coach I've certainly achieved a reasonable level of success. As a husband and a father I've done okay, too. And I'm a great friend. But I'm still "in between." I need to be a better coach. Maybe I can be a better communicator. Maybe I need to listen more: in between. Our family is even in between. I can be a better husband and dad: in between. I can manage my time even better and stay in touch with more of my close friends: in between. I'm not yet where I want to be. Our team isn't where we want to be. We all have a higher place we'd like to be. We're all in between.

I also want to speak to people who are still "low," those who've not yet touched success but who know and believe in their heart that they can. They know they can do better than they've done and can do *much* better than many people around them expect. Those are the people who mean the most to my heart. I want them to feel confident in themselves and possess the tools to achieve their own dreams—no matter how "high" those dreams might be. We've all been low; we've all been near the bottom. We've all wondered at times whether we have the tools to succeed. I know I have, such as in high school when I was on the end of the bench and getting no playing time, at Cameron University when racist teachers wouldn't answer my questions, in the NBA when I was cut and had no idea if I would get signed, when I almost drove off the Mississippi River Bridge in an intoxicated stupor, when my parents died. Like you, I've been low. But thankfully, each time I was pulled out and upward and continued toward my goals.

More than anything, though, I want to reach anyone who

has dreams. And this is what I want everyone who reads this book to remember and embrace: Savor the journey. That's right; savor it. Enjoy every moment of your quest to aspire higher. Savor the process. Savor each day. That's the final "S" in my "S plan" that I've outlined in the second half of the book. In the first half of the book I gave you the tools to aspire higher: determination, discipline, and smart decisions. Now you have the strategy: raise your standards, your expectations for yourself and your behavior; create a system that will give you the best chance to maintain and reach your standards; take a stand for what you believe and what you will and won't embrace as acceptable behavior; and now you've got to savor the journey. You've got to savor every minute of the effort—every small step forward and even every setback. Savor it.

As much as I aspire higher as a coach and we aspire higher as a team, there's no guarantee we'll achieve our goal. Therefore, we find daily joy in savoring the process of aspiring toward that goal. We savor the road trips. We savor the Christmas parties and team dinners. We even savor watching films. We savor the victories, and we even savor the defeats. It's the journey. It's savoring the solid pass or the well-run play. It's savoring the charging foul or the offensive rebound in the final minutes. It's not just hoping to hit a shot to win the title, but savoring the one million shots you took in practice in preparation for the opportunity. The joy isn't only in making the big assist in a game; it's the thousands of passing drills that helped prepare you to make that pass. It's not just savoring the last-second block to preserve the win, but savoring the hours of film the player watched to understand the defensive player's tendencies and put him in the right place at the right time to make the play. That's what gets my juices pumped, knowing how hard my guys worked in an empty gym to put themselves in position to do what they do before the big crowds on game nights.

In your own life, savor every moment, every day. It's not just about the raise, the promotion, or the new job, but the process of obtaining it. It was the learning and the performing that lets you know you earned it. It's not just that your students got great grades on their finals, but the process of teaching them and seeing the "light" go on in the eyes of the one student who was having the most trouble. It's not just selling the home as a real estate broker but the process of getting a fair price and seeing the satisfaction in the eyes of both buyer and seller as they undertake such a significant change in their lives.

It's not just having a new baby, but the process of making the baby. Whatever the achievement it's not just the victory itself, but the joy of getting there.

In business the joy isn't simply when the company goes public; the joy is in the journey required to get there—the details, the financial successes, the challenges. It is creating the business plan, hiring the employees, and finding the right office space and making it reflect your corporate culture. It is interacting with clients and recognizing when one of your employees does a good job. It's not just when the company is featured in *The Wall Street Journal* or *Fortune* or on CNBC. The joy also comes in the days when there is no media around and you are working until four in the morning to get the numbers right. It's the journey.

One thing I miss about my days as an NBA player is being on the bus. Of course, I still ride the bus as a coach, but as a player it's totally different. As a coach, you're thinking about too many things: scouting reports, games, practices, playing time, new plays. Players have none of that responsibility. To them, being on the bus is pure fun. It's sharing time with your teammates in a way you can't anywhere else. I miss landing in a city, getting on the bus, and heading to the hotel with the guys. I miss taking the bus to the opposing team's arena, or going to practice on the road. There's just something about the bus. You laugh, you joke, you share. Sure, there were times when it was a bit more serious, but no matter what, you were sharing the experience with your teammates. I miss the fraternizing and the jokes, the guys trying to talk like me. Of all the guys I played with, Antonio Daniels did the best Avery Johnson impersonation, and David Robinson did the worst. He didn't sound like me at all—even though he thought he did. On the Mavs, Jerry Stackhouse probably does the best impersonation now. Man, if I miss anything about playing, it's that bus.

I also miss some of the testosterone-filled brushups I had with some of my opponents. Two guys I had the utmost respect for were Karl Malone and John Stockton of the Utah Jazz. Together Stockton and Malone were one of the best one-two combinations in the history of the NBA. I had a number of wars playing against those guys, during the regular season and in the playoffs. I learned a lot playing against them. I learned a lot about toughness, preparation, and physicality. No one can tell me those guys weren't special just because they didn't win a championship—no one. I remember one game—and I truly savor this memory—when we were playing them in Utah, and Malone set an illegal pick on me, which was the norm for him. I told the ref, "Hey, he's moving on the screen." Karl yells to me, "Shut the hell up and stop complaining." Mind you, we're still playing during this exchange. Of course I can't let that go. I yelled something back that's best not printed here; let's just say it was a spicy version of the word "wimp."

He started laughing and said, "Hey, I thought you were a preacher." "Don't sell me short, [_____]," I kept yelling. Even my teammate Doc Rivers rose off the bench and yelled, "Yeah, Karl, you are a [_____]!" I told him if he touched me again with an illegal screen I'd knee him in the, well, we'll say groin. He tried it again, and I kneed him in the groin. Hey, I said I would.

I love that guy; I respect him quite a lot. It wasn't funny then, but that memory cracks me up now. I barely shook hands with Karl and John during our pre-game captains' meeting at half-court, but I truly respect them both. Savor the journey.

You may be asking, Well, why *not* just savor the achievement itself? The danger in focusing on the destination rather than the journey is that there's a possibility you won't reach your destination. There's no guarantee we'll reach our goal of winning an NBA title. We're going to do everything in our power to reach our destination—we're busting our butts *every day* to get there, and there are no shortcuts—but there's no guarantee we'll arrive. That's why you must focus on each of the steps required to reach the destination. It's why you should enjoy the steps, so that if you don't achieve the specific goal you set out to reach, then you'll feel good about the things you accomplished along the way.

In truth, it's the steps that make you smarter, not the end result. The steps elevate your skills and develop your knowledge about the goal. Savoring the steps—the process—means you won't feel like your efforts were fruitless even if you don't accomplish exactly what you set out to do. It means you'll be better prepared for the next opportunity that may come along—something you may not have even thought about before. A lot of NFL fans forget that Indianapolis Colts head coach Tony Dungy was fired as head coach of the Tampa Bay Buccaneers a year before he was hired by the Colts. Tampa Bay was a step. Before that, he was an assistant coach for six other teams, including one college team. Steps. Before that, he played for the University of Minnesota and two NFL teams, Pittsburgh and San Francisco. Steps. In Indianapolis he built a team that was known for its exciting, high-scoring offense and its regular-season success. But in the playoffs, there was always disappointment. Steps. In January of 2006, he finally broke through; he won the Super Bowl.

I don't know Tony personally. We traded voice mails last year, and I donated to the fund created in honor of his son who committed suicide. I admire him from afar. I admire his steps. I admire the integrity and dignity he showed along the way, even as he was being criticized for shortcomings, rather than being celebrated for the success he'd already had. Throughout that period I remember hearing him talk about how much he enjoyed spending time with Peyton Manning, his star quarterback. They both wanted to get to the Super Bowl as much as anybody in the NFL. As they aspired higher, they savored the steps. They savored the process of winning and losing and growing. They savored their practices, their meetings, their film sessions, their plane rides, their time in the locker room. Their quest was not merely focused on the end result, it was about the journey.

I enjoy being around Dirk Nowitzki. I savor watching him get better, watching him develop his game, watching him develop into one of our leaders. I am savoring those moments with all of my players. One day during training camp this season, I spent a couple of hours shooting a "Got Milk?" campaign with Josh Howard, another one of our leaders. I enjoyed the time spent with him. There will be times when Josh drives me crazy, like all my players, but I savor the time I spend with him. I also savor his grandmother and mother's cooking when we're in North Carolina to play the Bobcats. They take special care of "Coach". Thanks, Mom and Grandma!

As I took each step in my journey, I always had a backup plan. As you've read, I was prepared to become a psychologist. If my basketball career stalled anywhere along the way, I was heading straight to Tulane to get my master's degree in psychology and then begin my career as a therapist. Your backup plan should be based on something that fits your passion and your skills. It shouldn't be so far-fetched that it's really a pipe dream that's all but unattainable. That only leads to frustration. What you want is a backup plan that gives you confidence that things will be all right even if plan A doesn't work out. To ensure that your backup plan is strong—and that you're a better manager, writer, teacher, doctor, or entrepreneur—take smart steps. You can have a higher destination, but be smart about how you plan to reach it, and always have an escape route. One of my favorite Bible stories involves three men— Shadrach, Meshach, and Abednego—and how they refused King Nebuchadnezzar's order to bow down to a golden idol created in the king's image. Nebuchadnezzar was livid. He was so angry that he ordered the three men be put in a fiery furnace if they continued to refuse to bow down to the statue. He was so angry that he ordered the furnace heated to twenty times its normal temperature. Shadrach, Meshach, and Abednego took a stand, but they also had a backup plan: their faith in God. They told the king, *You can take us out. We might burn, but we're still not going to serve you. No way.* The fire was so hot it killed the men who dropped them inside. The king was sure they were dead but when he looked into the furnace he saw Shadrach, Meshach, and Abednego *dancing around inside.* More than that, he saw a fourth man inside the furnace, an angel sent by God, who was protecting them from the flames. Now, that's a backup plan!

My backup plan now is simple: I'll continue to serve. I'm enjoying the journey. I enjoy just talking with the guys and serving God. We may not get what we want but I'm still going to serve. If we don't win a championship and one of my players calls me during the off-season with something he needs, I'll still serve him. I'm aspiring higher, but I still have a backup plan, and it's to continue to serve.

When I was younger, I used to love to eat snowballs; you probably call them snow cones. Most people like the last slurp when the syrup is at the bottom of the cone. Not me. I liked to get the grape and orange all mixed together, and mixed together, and mixed together until I got it just right. What I savored was not just that last sip, but all the sips and spoonfuls of my own special grape-orange flavor along the way. Enjoy your own "snowball" moments—not just the start of the journey when you're excited and hopeful and everything is possible (when the snow cone is pretty), and not just at the end (when you get to the syrup)—savor every bite in between.

Aspiring higher can be intense. It can be tiring, with the long hours required to study more, do research, or simply manage all of the necessary details, so savoring the journey isn't always easy. It can be hard to savor the day-to-day steps when you're often just struggling to take the next step. But here's a trick that'll help you find the time and energy to savor the tasks: smile. Have some fun. Sounds simple, doesn't it? Well, it's not. We all forget to smile. In our focus and our determination, we just forget to smile. That's one of the things I have to remind myself of. I'm such an intense person. I have to maintain my focus in order to be successful. But at least once every day, I try to smile. Not just for a second or two, but for a long, enjoyable moment. I try to remember something I really enjoyed—a family vacation, some time with my kids, a particularly funny moment in the locker room, a good joke. In 2006–07, one of our players,

Austin Croshere, was having a pretty tough year. He signed with us as a free agent but had a tough time fitting in, and by December, he wasn't getting much playing time. He played only one minute in a game against the Los Angeles Lakers in January, and scored two points, hitting his only shot. Two nights later, against Seattle, he was a completely different guy. Or maybe he was the same guy—the guy who hit his only shot against the Lakers. Austin hit eleven of fourteen shots and scored thirty-four points—his season high—in just twenty-four minutes. He also had seven rebounds and three assists. The guy was impersonating Larry Bird! We won 122–102—not one of our best defensive games—but we won. Right after the game, I asked Al Whitley, our equipment manager, to find me an Austin Croshere jersey. I walked into the locker room wearing his jersey and the guys cracked up. He's 6'10" and well, I'm not. I looked like a kid inside a tent. The guys told me I needed to work on my biceps and triceps. It was all in fun. Austin was having a rough year. He wasn't enjoying this part of his journey, I'm sure. But I just wanted to show him we all loved him and were happy for him.

I've just got to smile. I've got to find some joy every day. Without it, the day's just a day and I work too hard to let that happen to any day. Find a way to enjoy yourself today. Even as you're focused and intense, find a way to smile or, if you're lucky, laugh. You can't be serious all the time. I'm forty-two, turning forty-three in March of 2008, and I don't want to look my age, so I try to smile as much as I can. A smile always makes you look younger. And it's not only good for you, but it's good for others, as well. It's like a light that shines, one that lifts others as well as you. The Bible says, "Let your light shine." It's amazing what a smile can do.

I try to interject some levity into practices every once in awhile—when I sense the team needs it. Maybe we'll play shooting games for fun rather than run drills. The guys have to buy the winner lunch or dinner. Every now and then, I'll play a shooting game with someone on the team—that's always good for a laugh—or maybe we'll go to a movie rather than practice. I love our team lunches and dinners on the road.

All of this helps us savor the journey. It helps to put us in the right spirit. Nothing you've read in this book works if you're not in the right spirit. More than anything, that means being balanced. We all get out of balance at times. We overemphasize work, for instance, or we overemphasize socializing. We can overemphasize anything at the expense of something else that is equally important. How many intense people in the finance industry overemphasize studying the market and analyzing data at the expense of working out or spending time with their families? Unbalanced. I can be pretty intense, so I'm trying to read more. I'm trying to take a few more vacations with the family. I go to the driving range to work on my lousy golf swing. I work out more, trying to take my 20 percent body fat down to 14 percent. I'm trying to be in the right spirit. Balanced.

Another way I get in the spirit is by doing charity work. I love helping to feed the homeless. I'm involved with an organization in Dallas called Hunger Busters and I love my time with them. Okay, most of the people we feed tell me how to coach the team, but I still love it. People come to the trailer for a bag of chips, a sandwich, and an apple and seeing them puts me in the right spirit. It keeps me in a giving spirit.

Long ago, I asked myself the question: Why do I exist? My answer was clear: I exist to serve. I'm here not to be served but to serve—to serve my family, my coworkers, my friends. I'm here to serve them all first. One of the easiest things I can do to serve them is to smile. There are times I need to be serious with all of them, but our relationships thrive when there is balance. Each emotion needs the other. I know I've got to serve. I've got to serve constructive criticism when it's needed. I know I've got to serve contracts. I've bought cars for family and friends. And it's always good to serve up a smile. My wife and I got married in 1991. We met when we were both at Southern, so we've known each other for the majority of our lives. I hear some men today say they don't want to get married until they're fifty, and it kills me. Guys, reexamine that thought. I wanted to get married while I was still in the NBA so someone else could savor the journey with me. I hear today's young players talking and nobody wants to get married. Some don't want to share their new money; others just don't want to give up the lifestyle. At the heart of it, though, is that a lot of these young men don't want to make a commitment to anyone but themselves. People, in general, don't want to be committed. The evidence is all around us with the rise in single-parent households and the divorce rate. Commitment is an endangered species, and it's a shame.

Share your wealth. Share your resources. Share your home. Share your car. (Hey, these material things aren't going with you anyway. After you're gone, someone else will be driving your car, living in your home, and spending what used to be your money, so share it while you've still got it!) Share your knowledge and your wisdom. Share your status and your popularity. Share it with somebody and you might be surprised how much more fruitfully it comes back to you. A few years ago I took my wife's niece, our godchild, and her brother on a big trip to San Diego and Las Vegas. I had fun, but the real joy was in sharing that time with some of the people I care about. My wife and I have taken people to Hawaii, we've taken friends and family to games and to the Finals when I was a player and then a coach. Allow someone to share that journey with you. That's why I like to keep tickets with me. I've given some out to people I meet on the street. I like to give them away at restaurants and at the cleaners. When I go to schools to speak, I like to give out tickets. You've got to share the journey. Every now and then I might invite a little kid out of the stands to come into the back and meet players. Share the journey. There are a lot of young people who've come up to me and mentioned that they were in one of my camps when they were younger. They mention something I said at the camp, and tell me how they incorporated it into their lives. That makes me go higher.

Sharing your journey with young people is like planting seeds that you hope will blossom and then reseed for others. What you say to them can be powerful. One night I met two of our season-ticket holders, John and Rick, two bigwigs from Coca-Cola. We decided to go to dinner but the night we picked was on the same night of John's parent–teacher conference. His daughter was in high school, but she remembered me coming to one of her camps several years before. I don't remember the exact message I gave that day, but I always say to kids, Work hard, play hard, pray hard, and no excuses. When she heard his dinner plans with me conflicted with the conference, she said, "Let mommy go to school, and you go have dinner with Avery Johnson. What he said at my camp was unbelievable." I get that kind of stuff all the time, and it warms my heart. I've helped put on a camp in Laredo since 1999 where we host about 2,000 kids every summer in six different locations. Many are Mexican and Hispanic kids who are always being scrutinized because of the immigration drama going on in this country. Not long ago, I met a woman who works for a friend of mine. She said she used to attend the camps in Laredo and told me how much the experience helped her to become a productive adult. Like I said, it warms my heart. What you say to anyone who aspires to be where you already are can be powerful. So savor your speech. Savor the words you use whether in public or in private, whether to a group of 4,000 or to your spouse in the privacy of your own home. In fact, as you rise personally and professionally, your privacy decreases in proportion. And I'm not just talking about those of us who live in the public eye. No matter who you are and where you are in your journey, remember this: somebody's always watching.

Somebody's watching to see how you handle prosperity and power. Somebody's watching to see how you handle pressure and disappointment. Somebody's watching to see how you change as you rise, or as you fall. Somebody's watching to see how you handle your kids, or your spouse. Somebody's watching to see how you treat the people who serve you. Somebody's watching to see how you *lead*. Your children are watching, your spouse is watching, your coworkers are watching, your boss is watching. People who you don't know are watching. Somebody's always watching.

At Southern, Coach Jobe used to write things on pieces of paper, then stick them in his pocket. In practice he would suddenly write something down and stick it in his pocket. During games, on the road, in restaurants, anywhere—he'd write something down, then stick the piece of paper in his pocket. I didn't find out what it all meant until the end of my junior season. At the end of the year, he'd call you into his office to tell you whether or not your scholarship was being renewed. That's when I learned he was writing down all of our transgressions. Anytime a player mouthed off to a coach or acted rude in a restaurant or on a bus, or was late for practice, or missed a study hall—Coach Jobe wrote it down. And when he called you in he'd pull out a clear plastic bag with your name on it. Inside were all of the pieces of paper on which he'd written things down about you. If your bag was filled with strips of paper, you could bet you'd hear, "Son, your scholarship is cancelled."

I went in confidently. I felt like I'd been very subordinate and submissive. Okay, not all the time, but even when I wasn't, I wasn't rude. I'd been a great kid. I'd already been coaching behind the scenes, so I was not worried at all. And in fact, my bag contained only one slip of paper. It said, "Great job, Coach." He was complimenting me. So my meeting lasted only two seconds. Some of my teammates didn't make it. He told them their scholarship was cancelled and they had to find another school. Somebody's always watching.

Share and savor the journey. What a lonely feeling it must be to reach your destination and discover that you're there by yourself; you've got no family, no friends, no people who are genuinely happy for you. Perhaps you've been selfish or simply so sold out to the goal that you forgot to be sold out to others. You forgot to serve others and simply served yourself. What's to savor in that?

Maybe that's why a lot of successful people commit suicide—literally (sadly) and figuratively. They feel lonely and alone and suddenly discover that what they were chasing wasn't all they thought it would be. That reckoning can kill the passion that sparked the journey in the first place. And it certainly can kill the spirit.

If you're fortunate, though, the destination will be everything you hoped for—and more. My "destination" as a player was winning the NBA championship. Some small-minded critics say our championship had an asterisk because we won at the end of a season that was shortened by the lockout of the players by the league during negotiations over a new collective bargaining agreement. Instead of a regular eighty-two-game season, the 1998–99 season was shortened to fifty games. But you know what? We won four series to win the title—the same number of series the eventual champions have to win every season. Plus, we earned a *full* playoff share. We didn't get a piece of a championship trophy. I have the whole ring. A lot of people tried to place *insignificance* on the Spurs' *significant* accomplishment. But we still savored the season, and we especially savored the championship. I savor the moments with teammates Steve Kerr, Jerome Kersey, and all the others. I savor having watched David Robinson win his first championship. For years we heard about all these great players like David who never won a title, so it was great to see him finish a season with a win. Tim Duncan was so happy for him. Sure, he and the other young players were happy for me, Sean Elliott, and the other veterans. But they were especially happy for David. In his own way, David was overwhelmed with joy, but he was still humble. I savor having seen Mario Elie going out to a club that night in his uniform and dress shoes. We laughed so hard when we saw him, but he didn't care. He just said: "I'm not getting dressed. I'm not taking this off." I savor that memory.

For me, winning the title was not just for Avery Johnson. It was for all the people who helped me on that journey. It was for all the people who invested in me. The shot I hit from the corner came with about forty seconds to go. The play was called "Four Down." It was for Tim, but we couldn't get the ball to Sean, who was supposed to get it to Tim. So Sean curled and went to the top of the key. I got the ball to Tim but he was double-teamed. He got it to Sean, who penetrated and kicked it out to me in the left corner. I didn't have time to think about it because the twenty-four-second shot clock was in a "911" situation. So I just shot. It felt good. It felt like I was shooting all those shots back when Kenny Smith was working with me in Houston. It felt like I was shooting all those shots during the summer. I wasn't the first, second, or even the third option on the play. But I felt God had me well prepared to take that shot. I just had to knock it down.

I didn't know it was going to be the last basket. But we got a stop, they got a stop, then Knicks guard Latrell Sprewell—a former teammate at Golden State—missed a shot over David and there was pandemonium.

Decide today to savor today because tomorrow is not guaranteed. Commit to aspiring higher, but even more importantly, commit to savoring and sharing the journey. Don't forget that there will be storms, times when your high aspirations will seem farther away than they did before your journey began. There are no slam dunks or easy layups for anyone who aspires higher. But there can be joy in every step. I tell my players to enjoy running up and down the floor against the worst team in the league in the dead of the winter part of the season. Enjoy being in the game, or even on the bench. Enjoy being at practice and, of course, being on the bus. Enjoy being *in the hunt*.

I won my championship as a player, but I haven't yet as a coach. Losing in the 2006 Finals was painful for everyone in our organization, from our owner down to the last guy who locks the doors at night. But I told my team, "Would you rather be a team that's never been in the Finals, or would you rather be in the hunt like the Buffalo Bills, who lost three straight Super Bowls?" I'd rather be in the hunt like the Bills because at least they *got there*. If we're in the hunt, we're going to break through. You can't win the Super Bowl unless you get there, and the Bills have gotten three chances so far. That's three blessings. I'd rather have chances like the Utah Jazz, who also never won the title, or the Portland Trail Blazers, who won a championship in the 1970s, and who had chances in the 1990s but didn't win. At that point you've got a 50–50 chance to win it all. As painful as it might be to lose the game, I'd rather take my shot than not get to taste it at all.

That's why I tell people what a blessing the 2005–06 season was for us, even though we lost in the Finals. It looked *really* good after what happened the next year, though the 2006–07 season was a blessing to savor, as well. I'll get there and take my chances over not getting there any day. And as much as I savor the journey of training camp, preseason, regular season, and then the playoffs, I also savor every practice. I savor that moment when I'm showing a young man something and he finally gets it. It might be a bounce pass or an offensive cut, and when he gets it in a game. But that moment when he gets it—man!— what a special feeling. We might not even win the game, but I'll savor that very small victory with that young man because we may have been working on it for weeks. And it will help us win games later on.

Last season, Jason Terry, our starting guard, had been working on an in-and-out offensive move every day. He was so happy when he finally scored on that move in practice. Just seeing the joy of accomplishment in that young man's face was something to savor.

Why do we exist? In my mind, we exist to live and give. Aspiring higher is how to live. Aspiring higher is striving for everything we're capable of achieving. Aspiring higher is finding your gift and sharing it with others. Aspiring higher is being determined, disciplined, and making smart decisions. Aspiring higher is standing through the storms in your life. Aspiring higher is challenging yourself to be a better person tomorrow than you are today. Aspiring higher is setting new standards to live by, creating sound systems for meeting those standards, taking a stand when the time comes, and—more than anything else—aspiring higher is savoring every step of the journey.

I've told my wife that when I die, I want her to put on my tombstone: "He Was A Giver." I want to be remembered as a giver of time, money, wisdom, love, advice, direction, and counseling; a giver. I want it to say: *Avery Johnson was a giver.*

If you want to go higher, give: to yourself, to life, to everyone.

NINE

You Are Destined to Win

CONGRATULATIONS! YOU'RE ALMOST FINISHED with this book, which means you now have the tools and strategies to aspire higher in your life. There's only one thing left to do: Get to it! Reading *Aspire Higher*—or any book that inspires and motivates you—is a great start. Obtaining critical information is one of the key components in creating a system (remember?) that will allow you to achieve your dreams. But once you close these pages, what are you going to do next?

Here are my thoughts, organized alliteratively once again to help you remember them, around "E" words: be *excited* about life, *expect* to win, *exchange* negative thoughts for positive ones, *elevate* your dreams, *eliminate* bad influences and envy, *evaluate* your gift, *educate* yourself, strive for *excellence,* become an *expert* manager. All these ideas are designed to point you toward *excelling* at *excellence.*

A lot of motivators preach excellence. That's the standard for any high achiever in any field. Success does not come without excellence. At first glance, you might think the idea of excelling at excellence is redundant. Not at all. Not one bit. Watch me now: If you have truly big dreams, excellence may not be enough. It'll certainly get you higher. It will get you good grades in school. It will get you good reviews at work and may actually get you that promotion. Excellence will help you write a solid business plan and it might even get you the spouse of your dreams. But the reason you picked up this book isn't merely to be excellent. You want to win. You want to win and you know that excellence may not be enough. It's not enough in the NBA. Several teams are excellent. There are several excellent coaches and a lot of excellent players. So it takes more than excellence to win an NBA title. NBA champions excel at excellence. It takes all the things outlined in these pages, and then some.

It takes more than excellence to transform an idea or a passion into a business. It takes more than excellence to lift the GPA of an entire classroom. It takes more than excellence to go from being a car salesman to owning several dealerships. It takes more than excellence to climb Mount Everest. It takes more than excellence to truly touch people and transform their lives as the pastor of a church. All these things require you to excel at excellence. They require you to stand apart from your competition. They require you to rewrite the blueprint created by someone else. Aspiring higher requires you to excel at excellence. Winning requires you to excel at excellence. Winning begins with attitude. It begins with being *excited* about life. Before you can even think about winning, you must be enthusiastic about life. When you wake up each morning you have to be excited about getting out of bed and having yet another opportunity to win. Sure, there are realities, and some challenges, you may be facing. Your sales haven't been where you want them to be. Your competition is breathing down your neck. The numbers aren't quite right from the last quarter. Your child is struggling in school. Your back is sore. Your boss is a pain. There will be realities and challenges but when you open your eyes each morning, you must be enthusiastic about that particular day and the possibilities it offers you to win. Winners are just excited with who they are and where they are at that particular moment, and they're enthusiastic about the possibilities.

Winners also *expect* to win. When they step out of the door, when they step into a meeting for a presentation, when they step into the classroom for a test, when they go on a sales call: they expect to win.

You have to expect to win. As a team, we have to expect to win every night we step onto the court. Yes, we prepare. We lift weights, we practice, we study films, we eat right, but when we step onto the court, we have to expect to win or all that hard work and preparation means nothing.

I was one of the shortest players ever to play in the NBA. In the history of the league, no player under six feet tall played more games than I did, which was 1,050 games. When I walked onto the court, even though I saw giants, I expected to win.

Next, you must *exchange* negative thoughts for good ones. The battle to win doesn't start with your physical attributes or your physical skills. It starts in your mind. So you must exchange any negative thoughts you might have for positive thoughts. You must think positive thoughts. If you don't, all that excitement, enthusiasm, and expectations are deflated and useless. Negative thoughts will kill your enthusiasm in a heartbeat. Winning starts in your mind. Exchange those negative thoughts. Think victory, not defeat. Think about soaring not sinking. If you're a student, think about graduating, not flunking. In golf they talk about swing thoughts. If you step up to the tee and think about all the bad places the ball can go, into the water or into the woods, you might hit the ball too fat or too thin, or you might slice it or hook it. If you think about all those negatives, you are guaranteed to have a negative result. But if you think about driving that sucker three hundred yards down the middle of the fairway, or if you think about bending it around the dogleg just where it needs to be you have a much better chance of achieving it. Well, if you're like me you STILL might not hit it right, but if you don't have a positive thought you won't have a positive result. Negative thoughts never produce positive results, so exchange those negative thoughts for positive ones.

When I was at Southern University, one of the classes I had to pass for my major was Psychology Research. The teacher was a mean old woman, and she did not like athletes. She told me,

"Avery, you're going to have a problem graduating because you're going to have a problem passing Psychology Research. Do you understand that?" I knew she did not like athletes, but I was still surprised she would just assume that I would have trouble in her class. I responded, "No, I don't understand because I know I can pass your class." Thankfully, I did, and I graduated. It starts in the mind.

Exchange negative thoughts for positive ones if you are going to win. Doing so will *elevate* your dreams. As I've written, I always dreamed big dreams, even while growing up in the Lafitte housing projects in New Orleans. I always thought big thoughts. I *saw* myself doing what I am doing today. I elevated my dreams beyond my surroundings—surroundings that said a Black man had almost no shot at success. My career as a basketball player and a head coach started with a thought. It started with a dream. Don't let anybody diminish your big dreams.

You might have to make changes in your *environment*. Wherever you live, whomever you hang out with, whomever your friends may be, they are all part of your environment. Becoming a winner usually means having to change some things in your environment. I say this all the time: If nothing changes, then nothing changes. The Mavericks have made many environmental changes in order to achieve our new, elevated dream of winning an NBA championship. We had to change. We haven't arrived there yet, but we are in the process of continuing to make the changes necessary to get to that level.

Now we're starting to get to the hard part. When you are making the necessary changes to your environment, you just may have to *eliminate* some people. If negative people are constantly speaking negative thoughts into your ears they will affect your ability to win. They will affect your enthusiasm and your excitement. They will affect your dreams. Eliminate them from your environment.

As a kid, I ran around with a lot of people who wanted to drop out of school. There were a lot of kids who wanted to try selling drugs. There were a lot of kids who said, "Man, Avery, you ain't gonna *be* nothin', so stop trying!" I had to eliminate those people from my environment, even though some of them were my friends. They had to go.

Surround yourself with positive people. In the work environment, there are people who love to gossip. They love to gossip about the boss, about their coworkers, even about their clients. *He's not good enough. She's not good enough. They ain't all that.* Last summer, someone even tried to tell me that my boss, Mark Cuban, wouldn't do well on *Dancing with the Stars*. I disagreed. Hey, I'm not dumb. You can't gossip about *my* boss.

Let's be real. The need to eliminate from your environment is not always external. You may also have to eliminate bad habits or bad behaviors of your own. We all have some. I know mine, and you know yours. We must take a self-inventory and determine what *we* must do to win. I learned at the tender age of forty-two that we all have two habits we need to *stop* doing, two habits we need to *keep* doing, and two habits we need to *start* doing. Ask yourself where you are and, if you're not satisfied with the answer, take an honest look at your habits. Chances are that there are habits that got you there and, most importantly, habits that will keep you where you are. There may be some habits you must eliminate if you are going to win.

Here's a bad habit most of us need to work on eliminating: *envy*. One of the things I tell my players is that they have to eliminate envy. If a teammate is getting good, positive press, if a teammate gets on an all-star team, or is named player of the month, you must support that person because we are a team. We're all in it together: the good and the bad. If a teammate gets the glory, we all get a piece.

Don't be envious of coworkers or a friend who may be enjoying more success than you. If they're doing well in life, exchange envy for this thought: "I'm next." Maybe you aren't where you want to be right now; maybe your coworker or friend is where you want to be. Maybe they have the job you want, or they're able to afford the car, the clothes, or the vacation you want. Exchange the envy and say, "I'm next. I'm next in line."

Once you've shed envy and stopped coveting what someone else has, you have to *evaluate* your own gift. You probably already know your area of expertise. But some of you might be trying to pursue another path because you think you'll make more money, or maybe because you think it's "cooler" than what you're doing now. If you want to win, you must evaluate your particular gift. Ask yourself some tough questions: Am I really good at this? Is this really my gift? Is this what I am called to do?

If you're comfortable with your gift, you must still ask yourself: Is this an area in which I need major improvement? In the NBA I was what they call a "penetrator." I was quick and had very good ball-handling skills—good "handle" as the kids say—so I could dribble through the defense and get to the basket. I could penetrate the opposition. Once I got to the basket, I was pretty good at shooting layups, but when I couldn't get to the basket, I was not good at jump shots. So teams focused on trying to keep me from penetrating, to keep me away from the basket and force me to shoot jump shots. I had to evaluate my gift—playing basketball—and I decided I needed to get better at it. I had some help coming to that conclusion: One of my coaches, John Lucas, told me something I'll always remember: "Do you want the kind of money that jingles, or do you want the money that folds?" I thought it might have been a trick question, because the answer was obvious. "I prefer the money that folds," I told him. He said, "Well, you'd better get a jump shot." That's when I began to shoot five hundred jump shots a day, a thousand jump shots a day, until my arm was about to fall off. I never became a great shooter, but I got to the point where I had a little bit of a reliable jump shot. I evaluated my gift and decided I needed to improve.

After you evaluate your gift, *educate* yourself. Call it continuing education. Let's say you already know your gift. You may even be excellent at it. But if you want to excel at excellence, you may need to know even more about where you want to go. Find out exactly what it takes to get where you want to go, and then find out what it takes to excel once you get there. Look for people who are doing what you want to do, at the highest levels, and pick their brains. Dallas Cowboys owner Jerry Jones said in the

Foreword for this book that when he was just starting out he called successful people to ask if he could come talk to them. It may sound bold, but now he does that for other people who want to pick *his* brain.

Educate yourself. You may want a raise. You may want a promotion. You may even want to leave your job and start your own business. But understand that with the raise comes a rise in responsibility. The higher you go in any profession, the more you need to know. The higher you go, the more you will need to find solutions to major problems.

I hear it all the time from my friends: former NBA teammates and competitors: "I can do what you do." I say,

Can you really? I have to find solutions to major challenges because our standards, our expectations are so high. Do you really want to study like I do, and get to the office when I get to the office? When we were players we could get in at 10:30 a.m. and be home by 1:00 p.m.. But when you are a coach, you basically have to live in the office. I have a residence in Dallas but I pretty much live in the American Airlines Center where we play. You may see my salary. You may see my nice suits. But do you really want my problems? I have all-star problems sometimes, tough problems that need tough solutions. Those solutions require a real commitment to study more and be smarter than you have to be as a player. Can you really do what I do?

Sometimes that shuts them up. Sometimes.

Strive for *excellence*. This might seem obvious, but you'd be surprised how many people believe they're striving for excellence when they are really settling for mediocrity. They're fooling themselves instead of striving for and demanding excellence from themselves. I tell my kids all the time, "You can't be mediocre. You've got to strive for excellence."

I go to a lot of Avery Jr.'s basketball games. I really try to stay on the sidelines and not get too involved (my wife, Cassandra, does enough of that). But one of the things that brings me off the sideline is when my son is not giving his best effort. He may miss a shot or make a bad pass. It's basketball, those things happen. But I cannot accept a mediocre effort. You have to strive for excellence—strive to excel at excellence—in *every* area. Successful people don't aspire to be average. They strive to excel. They strive to set a new standard.

Years ago, when I was a player, we signed a guy who was supposed to be my backup at point guard. When I met him for the first time at training camp, he said something very interesting. Instead of saying, "Hey, A.J., I'm so glad to be your teammate. I want to learn from you and someday be where you are," he said, "Man, I'm here to take your job." I was stunned. I said, "What? You're gonna take *my* job? You just got out of college, son. I've been in the NBA for ten years and you're trying to take *my* job? What you *need* to do is become an excellent backup first."

Wherever you are right now, whatever your job may be, become excellent at it first. It's okay to desire a raise or a promotion. It's natural to want those things. But before you start demanding them, be excellent wherever you are. Be excellent at whatever you do now—then aspire for more. When you get there, you'll be better prepared to excel. You'll be better prepared to win.

Of course, you can do all these things and still not achieve the desired result. I love what a friend of mine said about his tennis game: Every time he made a bad shot, every time he missed a forehand or backhand that he knew he should have gotten, he quickly said to himself, "Next point."

I love that. Next point. We should all embrace that attitude when we hit a bump in the road. Next point. I didn't get the raise. Next point. I didn't get the promotion. Next point. No excuses. Next point. Whenever I am interviewed after a loss during the season, I try to never make excuses. When we lose, we lose. Next point. Next game.

We'll go back to the drawing board, we'll figure out what we didn't do well, and we'll do our best to get it right the next time. No excuses. Next point.

We didn't get it done as a team last year. We didn't reach our standard of winning the championship. This season we have another opportunity. No excuses. Next Point.

Winners also have to be *expert* managers. You may not have the title but you're already a manager. We all are. We have to manage just to conquer the day. The stay-at-home mom has to manage the carpool and after-school activities. Dad has to manage the relationship with his wife. The CEO and corporate vice president, of course they have to manage, but so does the bus driver, the teacher, the salesclerk, the waitress, and even the kid at the fast-food joint. They're all managers. Whatever you do, wherever you are, you're a manager. You already manage people, and you also manage problems.

To become an expert manager, you also have to manage challenges that may not be obvious. You have to manage praise, and you have to manage persecution. You have to manage power. At some point you may have to manage poverty. You may get fired. There may be no checks coming in, no money flowing into your bank account. But just as fast as you had to manage poverty, you may have to manage prosperity. You finally got that raise. You got that promotion.

And when all that happens, you must manage change. You may have to manage pauses in your life, times that feel like you're stuck in traffic. You must manage promises. Try not to make promises you can't keep. I have to manage my own feelings about people who've broken their promises and not kept their word to me.

You have to manage peace. Peace is good. There's nothing like peace on the pillow at night. But peace cannot always come from something external. Sometimes, it's got to come from within. I have peace about who I am and where I am in life. I have peace about my body, even though I'm trying to lower my body-fat percentage and manage my weakness for french fries and donuts. I have peace about my family.

When peace comes from within, when it comes from being enthusiastic and excited about life, when you expect to win, when you exchange negative thoughts for positive ones, when you evaluate your gifts, when you educate yourself, strive to excel at excellence, and become an expert manager, you are a winner. You walk like a winner, you talk like a winner, you think like a winner, you dress and behave and even exercise like a winner. You are designed to win, you were not created to lose. You were designed to win.

You are destined to win.

EPILOGUE

To Our Youth: Champions Under Construction

I CAN'T LEAVE THESE PAGES WITHOUT SPEAKING DIRECTLY to young people. I've spoken to thousands of you—boys and girls, teenagers and young adults—during my years as a player and coach, and many of you have told me how much my words of encouragement and guidance have inspired you. Well, you inspire me. Young people inspire me. You push me to aspire higher and to continue to be an example as so many adults were for me.

As you aspire higher in your own life, it's easy to be swayed and get discouraged. It's easy to get distracted by the gadgets at your disposal—the video games, the iPods, the laptops, the cell phones. It's easy to get lured by the many places you want to go—the movies, the mall, a friend's house, the street corner. It's very easy to get beaten down by the negativity of youth—the teasing and petty competitiveness; the lack of a clean, safe neighborhood; dangerous schools; and friends who seem dead set on achieving nothing.

Most of all, it's easy to believe "higher" is too far away from where you are to be realistic. Becoming a doctor, a business owner, a teacher, a chef, a landscaper, a firefighter, a judge, or a coach just might seem like it's too much work or just too many years down the road. Well, I'm here to tell you that you're already a champion. It's just buried deep inside you waiting to be nurtured and groomed and encouraged and prepared to win. Your gift has already been delivered and it's just waiting to be unwrapped. The desire to aspire higher makes you a champion, and the determination, discipline, and decisions you make today *and* tomorrow will determine your journey.

You are champions—champions under construction.

Look at yourself like a house—a home—you'd like to build. It's your dream home, something you've imagined for as long as you can remember. You want it to be memorable. You want it to be majestic. You want it to be the best house in the neighborhood. You want to be proud of it.

What is the first thing you need to build your dream home? Let's start with a blueprint. It's a guide, something that tells you exactly what you need to do. It tells you where every wall is to be built, where every window goes, where to put the doors. It tells you how large each room is and how they all fit together. In other words, it tells you everything you need to know to build your home.

For you, that blueprint comes from people who serve as examples of how you want to live your life. Maybe they do what you want to do. They're musicians, UPS drivers, doctors, pastors, dentists, or lifeguards. Maybe their family reflects how you want your own family to be. Maybe they simply live how you'd like to live. How they live their lives and how they got there can be your blueprint.

You need somebody that you can look up to and respect, someone whose life speaks to what it means to be champion. Some of you may think there are no such examples in your own neighborhood. Actually, there are; just look around. Your blueprint may be one of your parents. It may be your teacher. It may be your mail carrier, a local policeman, a member of your church choir. Different people can offer different examples of attributes, skills, and behavior you'd like to incorporate into your "house"— your life.

These blueprints may also come from the history books or the headlines. My blueprints were created from memories of my dad, but also people like Martin Luther King Jr. and Jesus. As I grew older, I looked at people like Ben Jobe, my college coach; NBA coaches Don Nelson, Pat Riley, and Gregg Popovich. Later, I looked for examples in other coaches, like Tony Dungy and Lovie Smith, men who not only represented the top of their professions but also strong men of God who were not ashamed to speak openly about their faith.

A lot of you might aspire to be professional athletes or entertainers. There's nothing wrong with that. Maybe your blueprint is outside these industries. Check out the story of President John F. Kennedy. He was an example for me. So was Bernard Griffin, one of my teachers. He was a champion to me. So is Ken Chenault, the CEO of American Express, Earl Graves, the founder of *Black Enterprise* magazine, and Oprah Winfrey, one of the most powerful and successful women in the world. Champions, all of them. Don't limit your own blueprint to what you see every day: look around. There are many examples of success and integrity that could be part of your blueprint.

When I built my house in Woodlands, Texas, just outside of Houston, I traveled all over the country looking at "championship houses" to see what they looked like. I wanted to see how big they were, what materials they used, how they were decorated, what special touches they had. So my dream home started as a blueprint that included much of what I liked in other houses. It didn't include things I didn't like; I saw plenty of those. Some things you'll see in people are traits you don't want to incorporate into your own blueprint. Those people can be "examples" too; examples of what you don't want to be.

Once you have your blueprint, you'll need to build a solid foundation. Without a solid foundation, the house isn't worth a nickel. Without a solid foundation, it'll leak. Without a solid foundation, the house will fall. Most solid foundations are built with stone or brick—anything strong and impenetrable that will stand the test and challenge of time. Your foundation should be built on having a solid character. Be a boy or girl of integrity and honesty who speaks well and has a good attitude. Those characteristics will weather any storm. Those characteristics never wear down or grow weak. Integrity and honesty are traits of champions.

Have a strong character because character is the foundation of a good name. In the Bible, Proverbs 3:3-4 says: "Let love and faithfulness never leave you; bind them around your neck, write them on the tablet of your heart. Then you will win favor and a good name in the sight of God and man."

Yes, there should be a spiritual element to your foundation. I can't tell you what kind of church to attend or what your own personal faith should be, but have faith in something other than—greater than—yourself. Have faith in a power that granted you your gift and that will guide you through the journey. Have faith in something that loves you and will be your rock, your shield, and your light. Trust me; that faith will take all the pressure off.

There are two other elements that are part of a solid foundation. One is academics. I won't be the only one in your life who'll tell you how important it is to do your best in school—or at least I hope I'm not. I can't describe how important school is. Yes, there are successful people in every profession who did not do well in school, but they are very few. There are many more successful people who did do well in school or who at least did their best. Play the odds in your favor. Take a stand and say, *I will not be a dropout.* Take a stand and say, *I will not be a quitter.* Academics are something you can stand on.

The final element of a strong foundation is friendship. You

don't have to have a lot of friends. In fact, you may not understand this now, but later in life you'll know that true friends are few. Right now most of the "peeps" you think are your friends are really just acquaintances. Later you'll probably have only a handful of true friends; people you can trust, people who have your back, people whose backs you'll have. Friends. There's nothing wrong with having a few good friends, and they don't all have to look like you. In fact they *shouldn't* all look like you. No matter where you live, the world you're growing up in is more diverse than at any time in America's history, and it's only getting more diverse every year. By the time you enter the workforce, corporate America may finally look like the rest of America. No group is going away. So get at least a few friends who don't look like you, people who are outside your current circle. Not all my friends are in basketball. I have friends in the oil and gas business. I have friends in financial services. I have friends who buy and sell companies. I have friends in education. I have friends in the theater. I have friends who are magazine editors. Each of them brings a different perspective to my life—and I love it.

Expand your circle to include friends who don't look like you. They'll add different perspectives and points of view to your discussions and debates. And you'll be better prepared to compete in an increasingly diverse world.

Overall, don't try to have too many friends. They'll become too many voices in your head. Too many friends are too much to maintain, too many people expecting too much, too much drama. A few good friends are all you need.

Now, with a blueprint created from the best of the best, and a foundation built on character, spirituality, academics, and friendship, it's time to start putting up the walls. It's time to start building. It's time to start moving. Stick to the blueprint. Rely on what you learn from others. Follow the examples of champions you wish to emulate.

The walls and the rooms they enclose represent different aspects of your life: school, family, job, and friends. Each room is a different size and has its own characteristics. Some rooms are sunny, others are dark. Some rooms are comfortable and cozy, while others are cold. Some days, a few of the rooms may be clean and tidy, while others will be unorganized and filled with dust. You'll spend time building each room and, when the house is completed, you'll spend time in each room. Most days you'll spend more time in some rooms than others. You may ignore some rooms for days. You'll have favorites. One thing these rooms have in common is that they are each built on the solid foundation you created.

Inside the house, each room will be a reflection of you. Invest in each room. Invest in your investment. Invest by going to class each day with the attitude of a champion. Invest by learning proper etiquette: how to eat at a restaurant, or how to treat other people. Invest by learning how to dress appropriately—stylishly but appropriately. Invest by getting tutoring in your difficult classes. Invest by working out and eating healthy—by taking care of the "temple" that is your body. Invest by getting a summer job. Invest by volunteering at a local church or charity.

Invest by not smoking or using drugs. Invest by waiting until you're married to have children.

Of course there's a roof, and in many ways it's much like the foundation, only rather than being the rock upon which your house stands, it is your protective covering. It is the power upon which your spiritual beliefs are based. My faith lets me know that God is my protection in the storms and my light in the dark. Your covering should also include elder family members and mentors, people who speak life to you every day. They have nothing to gain and are sincerely committed only to your well-being. Soak up their wisdom. Soak up their stories. Like your roof, they and their wisdom will cover you through the storms you'll inevitably face in life.

The final component in building your dream house is the welcome mat. It may seem trivial after all the work that went into the blueprint, foundation, walls, and roof. But hear me out: What good is a dream house if you live in it alone? What good is a dream house if no one ever visits? Whatever I gain in life I share with others: money, time, counsel. I have been blessed, which obligates me to share my blessings with others. Once your house is built, once you've finished decorating and redecorating the rooms, open your front door and invite others inside—particularly those who may come along after you, those looking for their own blueprint for aspiring higher.

You are champions under construction. You are designed to win, designed to be a champion. You were not designed to fail. Let the champions of yesterday and today inspire you. Don't be held back by failures of the past or by where you come from.

What's done is done. Your journey is not about where you come from because you're going higher.

Your house is designed to last. It is not designed to be inferior. It is designed to be an example. Your house is a showcase and—like you—it is designed to be a champion. Now build it.

ACKNOWLEDGMENTS

So many people have invested in me and contributed to this book—so many people who have inspired and shaped and molded (and even scolded me when I needed that, too)—it would be impossible to thank everyone. Your hands are on each of these pages.

All my love and thanks to my family, especially my wife, Cassandra, and my kids, Christianne and Avery Jr.; and to my brothers and sisters in New Orleans and elsewhere.

Thank you, Mark Cuban.

Thanks to my assistants, Leslie Tracy and Andrea Niles. They get me where I need to be and tell me what I need to know.

Thanks Terdema Ussery, the Mavs president and CEO, for reintroducing me to Roy S. Johnson, my coauthor, and planting the idea for this collaboration.

Thanks Roy. What a journey it was. (And thanks to his family—his wife, Barbara, and kids, Edwyn and Missy—for allowing Daddy to disappear for a while.)

Thank you, Jerry Jones, for contributing such a powerful Foreword.

Much thanks to my friend, Derek Lafayette.

To the HarperCollins team: Steve Ross, Mary Ellen O'Neill, Pete Fornatale, Jean Marie Kelly, Paul Olsewski, Doug Jones, Laura Dozier, and Helen Song; thanks for believing in *Aspire Higher*. Thanks, too, for your professionalism and especially for pushing us to the end.

Richard Pine, our agent at Inkwell Management, thanks for being an all-star dealmaker.

And thanks to all my business friends who have *aspired higher* in their own lives, and who allowed me to interview them for this book.

Thanks to all the coaches—from Biddy Ball to the NBA—who shared their wisdom with me, and to all the ministers who lifted me.

A particularly grateful thanks to my New Orleans "family," those I know and those I've never met. Thanks, and may God's blessings rain upon you all.